J. H. Brockmann

Oddfellowship

Its Doctrine and Practice Examined in the Light of God's Word, and Judged by its

own Utterances

J. H. Brockmann

Oddfellowship

Its Doctrine and Practice Examined in the Light of God's Word, and Judged by its own Utterances

ISBN/EAN: 9783337250843

Printed in Europe, USA, Canada, Australia, Japan

Cover: Foto ©Lupo / pixelio.de

More available books at **www.hansebooks.com**

ODDFELLOWSHIP.

ITS DOCTRINE AND PRACTICE EXAMINED
IN THE LIGHT OF
GOD'S WORD,

AND

JUDGED BY ITS OWN UTTERANCES.

TRANSLATED
From the Original German "Christian and Ernst" of

REV. J. H. BROCKMANN,
Pastor of the Evangelical Lutheran Church of Fort Atkinson, Wis.

CHICAGO, ILL.
EZRA A. COOK & CO., PUBLISHERS.
1878.

PREFACE.

"THE influence of the Free Mason Lodges upon State and Religion, has been greater than the majority of the members have known and their opponents have supposed," says Dr. Niedner in his Church History, page 777. This judgment we transfer upon the Odd Fellow lodges, and certainly with justice, as these two bodies have one and the same doctrine, entirely the same principles. Great is the influence of the lodges, as far as we can discern it, but who knows how far it extends in reality, as so much of it is exercised wholly in secret? Many thousands are yearly drawn into the net of the lodge, therein inflated "with proper conceptions of their powers and capabilities," brought to the conviction that they, without Christ, "are capable of doing good," are directed to place their reliance upon themselves and the order, but estranged from the Church of God and the blessed Gospel. Who shall bear the blame? Certainly, for the most part, those who are led astray, themselves; but not these alone. Prof. Dr. Hengstenberg, in his book—"Free Masonry and the Evangelical Pastoral Office"—I, page 56, says: "No small part of the blame rests upon the Church and her Theology, which hitherto have cared too little about penetrating into the nature of the order, or portraying the same in a clear and convincing manner, and proving its incompatibility with the word of God." Of these many thousands, estranged from the Gospel by the influence of the lodge, up to the present time, as experience proves, very few have returned to the same. As, however, if they remain thus estranged from the Gospel, none of them can be saved, Lo 　certainly demands that we should do everything in our power both to save those led astray, as well as to warn those standing in danger, which is surely best done by examining the doctrine and principles of the order in the light of God's word. This it is that has been attempted in this pamphlet, whether successfully, those conversant with the subject must determine. Every criticism dictated by knowledge of the subject and kindly feeling, shall be thankfully made use of.

In order to give an opportunity to test the doctrines of the secret societies by the everlasting word of God, be this little book recommended to all members and friends of the lodge, as well as to all antagonists of the same.

May the faithful God accompany it with his blessing!

THE AUTHOR.

FORT ATKINSON, Wis., July, 1874.

FIRST DIALOGUE.

> Beloved, believe not every spirit, but try the spirits whether they are of God. 1 John, 4 : 1.

Christian. I am very glad indeed to see you, Ernest, as I have something I would like to speak to you about. You have resided in this country longer than I, and are better acquainted with its manners and customs.

Ernest. Well, what have you on your mind this evening, Christian?

Ch. I will tell you. I was in town to-day, where I met Maurice. After conversing a while about the harvest, the price of wheat, &c., he asked me if I did not feel inclined to join the lodge. To my question, what kind of a lodge it was, he answered, the Odd Fellows' Lodge. As I expressed my astonishment at the name "Odd Fellows," and showed no great desire to become "odd," he said that was merely a name, and little or nothing depended on it; we must look to the matter, and that was *good.* He then extolled the lodge in the highest terms; praised, in his loquacity, its endless benefactions, and added that the Lodge was the dearest spot on earth to him, and so forth. Now I would beg of you, if you are able, and know anything about it, to give me a particular account of the lodge, whether it is really something good or not. I have often heard about the Free Masons, that they have a covenant with the devil. If this should prove something of that sort, I would never join it.

E. What did Maurice say was good in the lodge?

Ch. Alas, I cannot remember the half that he said; but, among other things, he said that if I joined it and should be sick, I would receive three or five dollars a week, I do not remember exactly which; and I should also have night watchers, without paying for them.

E. Is that all that he said?

Ch. He said, too, that all the members of the lodge were moral men, and if everybody would join, the world would become a Paradise; but the parsons kept the people in ignorance, that they should not be enlightened. I believe he added something about widows and orphans, funerals, &c., but it is pretty much mixed up in my head. I would like to have asked him some questions, but you know, with his extraordinary loquacity, one can scarcely get in a word; besides, I had no time, and was thinking that, perhaps, in our evening talks, when we smoke our pipes comfortably together, you could help me to an understanding of the subject.

E. The good Maurice has given you too much to digest at once, without considering that the portion we administer must be adapted to the strength of the stomach.

Ch. I believe you are correct. If he had taken point by point, listened to and answered my questions, the matter would have been much clearer to my mind. But be so kind, and inform me, if you can, WHAT THE LODGE IS, and WHAT IS ITS AIM?

E. Very good; I will do so, and think I can, for I have been a member these ten years. Therefore—

Ch. What! you, too, an—Odd—Odd—Odd—Fellow?

E. Indeed I am, and think to remain one, for it is really something good, excellent and noble.

Ch. This is indeed news to me! You never told me anything of it.

E. Well, I am very much opposed to taking any and every

one into the lodge. We should first become acquainted with persons. When we have learned to know a man's character, to be moral and steadfast, then we can propose and accept him, but no sooner.

Ch. Aha! Then you did not consider me to possess a morally steadfast character, and that is the reason you never said anything to me about it!

E. Not for that reason. When you become acquainted with the nature and principles of our order, you will surely not censure me that I did not immediately on your arrival tell you all about it and ask you to become a member. And this is what displeases me in Brother Maurice, that he, without having any nearer acquaintance with you, at once asked you to join. Another thing that I dislike is, that he talks immediately against the parsons. True, there are some who work against our order, and keep the people in ignorance; but there are many others who have nothing against it, neither indeed could they, because its aim is good and praiseworthy; and of these, many a minister has already joined the order, and I hope many more will yet unite with it; I could also wish that our own minister would soon become a member. If many of them are opposed to the lodge, the more friendly-disposed cannot answer for it; therefore I think we should not immediately begin to rail at the parsons.

Ch. What! Is Maurice your brother? I never knew that.

E. To be sure, he is not my brother by birth, indeed, no relation of mine whatever, but still my brother, because he belongs to the same order; all who belong to the lodge, be they where they may, are among each other brothers; they recognize each other as such, stand by each other, and hold together in every respect as brothers.

Ch. Really! Then, perhaps, after all, it is something good! But, by my digressions, we have wandered entirely from the subject, and you have been prevented from telling me what the lodge is and what is its aim. You must know, if you have belonged to it for ten years. Please tell me.

E. Well, I think I can speak from experience. In ten years one can learn something. Neither did I let this time pass by unemployed. I have profited by the lodge in many ways, and have much to thank it for. Pay attention, then! The lodge is an association of purely moral men, of honorable, steadfast character. They have united together for the purpose of doing good wherever they can, particularly in the support of the needy, visiting the sick, burying the dead, helping the widow and educating the orphan. They obligate themselves to stand by each other in all positions and circumstances of life, to assist and to save each other when they are in danger.* In this way, all the lodges of our order, of which there are over 5000 in America, are united. Every one stands by the other, helps and promotes his interests wherever he can, and if one of them be sick, he receives weekly his appointed aid. If he needs night watchers, every night two brothers are there, who wait on him, moisten his fever-parched tongue with a refreshing drink, and alleviate his situation in every possible way. If he dies, they render him the last services of affection by closing his eyes, providing for the funeral, and seeing to it that it is solemnly performed. Yea, the lodge provides for the surviving widow and her uneducated children, takes care that they do not suffer want, and that the children's minds are stored with useful knowledge and their heart and will are properly trained. Further, the lodge endeavors, by moral suasion, to unite all hearts in Friendship, Love and Truth, to banish prejudice and superstition, envy and hatred; on the contrary, to promote harmony and concord. To make all men happy,—that is its aim. In short, *the lodge is a magnificent Institution of Charity.* And what could be more ardently desired, than that all should unite

---

* See Odd Fellows' Pocket Companion, page 13.

with it, in order that the benefits of this great benevolence should descend upon all! And this is what we endeavor to attain by our labors. Here I have given you, in a few words, to know what the lodge is, and what is its aim. Consider now whether you will join or not. Consider whether it is not a fine thing in time of need to draw your weekly support; whether it is not consoling in sickness, every night to have two careful watchers by the sick bed; whether it is not tranquilizing to every well wishing father of a family, to know that after his death his widow and his uneducated children are provided for in this cold world, where so little love is to be found! You have yourself a small flock, of which the youngest cannot yet even walk alone. Now think for a moment: should you die to-day or to-morrow, how would your mourning widow and your helpless orphans fare? Surely every one, particularly fathers of families, can do no better than to unite with this benevolent association. Choose now, whether you will be left in sickness without sympathy, aid, advice and comfort, or whether you will enjoy comfort, advice, aid and sympathy. Choose whether at your death, which may possibly be near, you will know your widow and fatherless children provided for, or whether they shall be exposed to wretchedness, hunger and want! Choose whether your dear Catharine, after your death, shall be enabled to live respectably, or whether she, perhaps forsaken by all, shall beg her own and her children's bread at the doors of unmerciful men! Choose, and the sooner you decide to join, the better! If you have an inclination to do so, I will propose you to the lodge.

Ch. Hallo! You are almost as much excited as Maurice was. I have never seen you so animated and eager before.

E. Yes, certainly; for such a good cause one can become excited, and one can't help being vexed when here and there people are still to be found who are opposed to it.

Ch. Well, I do not know what to say to it; but so much I do know, that I cannot yet join. Support in time of need is all very fine; to know one's widow and orphans will be provided for after our death, has also its consoling influence; but I do not understand as yet how it all hangs together and what more is connected with it. At all events, I must first become better acquainted with the matter, and examine it, else I might perhaps do something contrary to my conscience, which is governed by God's word.

E. It is nothing contrary to your conscience, for the lodge demands nothing from any one that is in opposition to his conscience.* But I am not at all opposed to your wish to become better acquainted with the subject, and I can also lend you a helping hand thereto. I have at home several books and a whole mass of publications, in which everything concerning the lodge is clearly laid down, which I will gladly lend you, if you wish to read them.

Ch. I am very glad of it, for I would like to learn more of this subject, and to test it thoroughly. Can you come to-morrow evening a while? You know that the way I am situated at home, I cannot well leave.

E. I think I can.

Ch. Then please bring the books along. The evenings, which are already pretty long and constantly growing longer, afford leisure for reading.

E. I will do so with pleasure.

---

* See Odd Fellows' Improved Manual, pp. 73, 96, 119, 140; Pocket Companion, p. 309.

SECOND DIALOGUE.

Search the Scriptures. John 5: 39. That ye may prove what is that good and acceptable and perfect will of God. Rom. 12: 2.

Ernest. Well, neighbor, how do you get along?

Christian. Not very well! Last night I could not go to sleep for a long while; what I had heard yesterday concerning the lodge made my head to whirl, and when, at length, I did fall asleep, I dreamed I was in the lodge, and saw all kinds of abominable forms and shapes, so that I was terribly frightened. And then—

E. That came, probably, from your speaking yesterday about the covenant with the devil.

Ch. Very likely And then it seemed to me as if I were dangerously ill. Two of the lodge brothers sat by my bedside, and when I wanted water, and could only gasp a few unintelligible words, they gave me strong brandy. I could not speak. Gradually I became weaker and weaker. I felt death grasping at my heart, and yet I could not die. Then the two brothers closed my eyes. In the terrible anguish, that perhaps I should be buried alive, I awoke and found myself bathed in sweat.

E. Well, dreams are but phantoms.

Ch. So I thought.

E. Have you considered the matter further to-day?

Ch. Yes. This matter and what I heard yesterday I could not get out of my mind all day, and came near having a great misfortune in consequence.

E. In consequence of it?

Ch. Yes. I harnessed my horses to the plough to finish off that last bit of land, but my mind was so engaged with the lodge that I neglected to finish laying on the harness upon the gray, which is the off horse. No sooner had I begun to drive, than the gray, being very skittish, became aware that something was amiss, became unmanageable, sprang to the left, and I received a terrible blow in the side from the plough, which knocked me down, and it was with difficulty that I could at last arise and hobble home.

E. What became of the horses?

Ch. They ran home, and took no further damage, but the plough is broken.

E. You might have been killed.

Ch. So I might

E. Think only. Had the misfortune been greater, had you become a cripple, or remained dead on the spot, how would your family fare now? I could not be easy, did I not know that my family were provided for.

Ch. I thought of all that, and thanked God, from the bottom of my heart, that he had so graciously averted the stroke.

E. Indeed I do not know how any father can rest, who does not know that his family is provided for after his death. I, at least, could not.

Ch. Certainly a father must do his duty and provide for his family. I think, too, that I have never neglected my duty in this respect, and will continue, so long as God lends me strength and grace, to care for them.

E. That is all right, but certainly not sufficient. You cannot, for instance, in several years to come, earn so much, even should harvests prove extraordinarily good, that your family can live without care. But you might be suddenly called away, and then they would be destitute. They would, however, be provided for, so soon as you join the lodge and pay the small entrance fee, the weekly, accidental, half yearly and annual contributions. This is, without question, the easiest way to provide for them, as I told you last evening.

Ch. Humanly speaking, this may all be very true; but it seems to me as if this manner of providing were not entirely free from setting our confidence in man, and as if one did not believe that that blessed God, in whose care we daily commend ourselves and our families in prayer, would not provide for the widows and orphans, as he has promised to do. But I will not judge about that If I can convince myself that it is good, I shall consider it to be my duty to join; for, to him that knoweth to do good, and doeth it not, to him it is sin." But—have you anything to do with religion?

E. No, we have nothing at all to do with religion. We let every one believe as he pleases. The order is only an association for aid and charitable purposes. What did you mean with your "but," you did not come out with it?

Ch. Yes, but I do not like to tell you.

E. Only come out with it.

Ch. Well, but you must not be angry with me.

E. By no means.

Ch. By my terrible dream I have really conceived a terror of the lodge. Tell me, have you actually a covenant with the devil?

E. Man, are you crazy? *I* a covenant with the devil? I am a Christian. I was born and bred in the Christian religion; have learned Luther's smaller catechism, besides many texts and hymns; go to church and to communion. And should I have a covenant with the devil? No, I did not expect that of you! What do you take me for? Did you ever find me a child of the devil? Tell me, if you know anything diabolical in me!

Ch. Well, well! Don't fly into such a passion. Come, let us first light our pipes. Here are tobacco and matches. —Does your pipe burn?

E. Yes.

Ch. Now dear Ernest, I do not say that you have a covenant with the devil,—I merely ask. It partly appeared so to me in my dream, and I thought I would inquire. To be sure, I was afraid you would be angry.

E. Well, I will not be angry with you; yet it does vex me to hear such conjectures, especially from a friend. No; I tell you our order is nothing more than a benevolent and mutual aid association. You may believe me, that it has already caused an extraordinary amount of good, has distributed many benefits, and accomplished many works of charity. Many widows and orphans would to-day, in grief and want, be begging their bread from door to door, yea, would have perished, had our order not taken care of them. We do not accept each and every one, least of all one who has proved himself to be a child of the devil; but only such as are upright and religiously inclined. To aid the brethren, to visit the sick, to alleviate their sufferings if possible, to comfort them; to provide for widows and orphans; in short, to make all men, were it possible, happy, is our endeavor!

Ch. In the course of the day, I have reflected much about what you said yesterday evening,—that the members of the lodge know each other as brethren, be they where they may. I do not understand that. Should you, for instance, move to another state, and there meet a man you had never before seen, could you know whether he was an Odd Fellow, without any one telling you?

E. Certainly I could.

Ch. How is that possible? You cannot see into his heart!

E. No, I cannot; but we have certain signs by which we know each other.

Ch. What kind of signs?

E. I cannot tell you; but you will learn to know them if you join.

Ch. Why can you not tell me?

E. Because the signs belong exclusively to the lodge, and we have *solemnly vowed* not to communicate these matters to others.

Ch. Really! Then you have secrets?

E. Yes.

Ch. But the Apostle says (Eph. 5: 12): "For it is a shame even to speak of those things which are done of them in secret." And the Lord Jesus says (John 3: 20): "For every one that doeth evil, hateth the light, neither cometh to the light, lest his deeds should be reproved." Are not your secrets, then, sinful?

E. They cannot possibly be sinful, because they contain nothing bad in them. They are merely signs of recognition, and there is nothing evil in that. I am firmly convinced you, too, have your secrets; I mean family secrets.

Ch. Then I am to conclude by this, that you carry your so-called family secrets into the lodge. So, perhaps the only difference would be this: that the families not belonging to the lodge keep those matters, which they do not wish every one to know, to themselves; while you, on the contrary, take such family matters into the lodge, and besides *these* lodge secrets, have no particular family secrets which you retain for yourselves!

E. By no means. You have entirely misunderstood me. The lodge has its own secrets, and these consist mainly in the signs of recognition, the ceremonies of installation, and the rules and instructions upon conferring the degrees. Besides, we have, as all other men, our private family affairs, which we keep to ourselves.

Ch. That looks very suspicious. Signs of recognition, which no one else knows or dare know, by which you recognize each other, although you have never met before! Secret ceremonies and rules, which no one outside of the lodge dare find out! I think, if your doctrines were really good, Love itself should prompt you to communicate them to others. Here the words of the Apostle occur to my mind: "For it is a shame to speak of those things which are done of them in secret." To be sure, I will not maintain that your secrets necessarily fall under this class, for as yet I know too little about them; but it seems very suspicious to me. Pray, why do you have these mysteries?

E. Because the order, without these secrets, could not fulfil its high mission; because we should be continually cheated, defrauded and deceived, and our benefactions would often be misused if we did not have these signs. Indeed the order cannot exist without these secrets. But why should I longer dispute with you and answer your thousand and one objections and scruples? You wanted to see the books. Here they are. Only peruse them with attention, and I am convinced you will find nothing evil in them. Indeed, your opinion of the order will be entirely changed, your prejudices will vanish, your doubts be removed, your disinclination be transformed into inclination. Yes, I rejoice in anticipation, my dear neighbor, of seeing you brought into the lodge.

Ch. I am glad you brought the books along. I cannot rest till I have examined the subject to its very foundation.

E. Do so. I tell you, the more you search into it and the more thoroughly you test it, so much the more beautiful will you find our lodge, so much the more noble its aim, so much the more lovely its communion. That is just where so many miss ... cause they do not examine into it. Would they only test our principles, many more would join us.

Ch. What are the names of those books?

E. This is our Manual. The title is: "The Odd Fellows' Improved Pocket Manual. By Rev. A. B. Grosch. Philadelphia: Th. Bliss & Co. 1869." I would recommend this especially to your attention. It is the best and most thorough of them all, and particularly recommended by sixty-seven Grand Representatives of the Grand Lodge of the United States, who affirm that this book is "a complete and faithful representation of the History, the Principles, Instructions, Work and Organization of the Order," and that we can rely upon its instructions "as correct." This other book bears the title: "The Odd Fellows' Pocket Companion. By James L. Ridgely. Cincinnati, O. R. W. Carrol & Co., publishers. 1868." This is also good, and enters more fully into the Constitution. This other is our Compendium, a collection of the Laws and Decisions of the Grand Lodge of the United States. The title is: "Digest of the Laws, Decisions and Enactments of the R. W. (Right Worthy) Grand Lodge of the United States, I. O. O. F. (Independent Order of Odd Fellows). 1871." (To be had of James L. Ridgely, Baltimore.) In this book you have not only our Laws, but also the Constitution, By-Laws and Regulations of the United States Grand Lodge, as well as the ceremonies at funerals, dedication of a lodge, &c. And, that you might thoroughly examine everything, I have also brought along the Constitution and By-Laws of our State and of our subordinate lodge, as well as a large bundle of transactions and resolutions of the United States Grand Lodge, the Grand Lodge of our State and of our State's Grand Encampment of different years, and a great collection of our periodicals.

Ch. That is certainly a great mass of reading matter; but I am very glad that I now have the opportunity to become acquainted with the subject from the best authorities. Are not all these books and papers written by members of the lodge?

E. Yes, each one of them, and what they contain is correct, on that you may depend. Only study them diligently.

Ch. Certainly I shall have enough to do for a while.

E. To be sure you will, and, that you may not lose any time, I will not disturb you for a time with my visits.

Ch. Well, that need not hinder you from coming.

E. I think it is better that you should not be disturbed.

Ch. Well, if you insist upon not coming for a while, I yet entreat you not to put off your next visit for too long a time.

E. Very well, it shall not be too long.

THIRD DIALOGUE.

> Know ye that the Lord he is God: it is he that hath made us, and not we ourselves; we are his people, and the sheep of his pasture. Ps. 100 : 3.
> (Isa. 44: 6. 1 Cor. 8 : 6.)

E. Well, dear Christian, how do you get along with your studies? Have you almost worked through the documents?

Ch Yes, day before yesterday I read the last page.

E. Indeed you have been very diligent!

Ch. Yes; when I have something of this kind before me, I cannot rest until it is finished. I also availed myself of several rainy days we have had to read.

E. Well, how does the thing please you now?

Ch. I cannot answer you in a few words.

E. Is the subject now clear to your mind, or have you still all manner of doubts and objections?

Ch. I believe it is now clear to me, for I have closely read all the documents. Many portions I have read over at least three times, and have carefully reflected on all. But I have some doubts, and must make many objections.

E. That is certainly more than I expected. What kind of doubts and objections have you?

Ch. I cannot set them forth in brief terms. We must take point after point. First, I must observe that you have stated the affair in a very different manner from what it is depicted in your own publications.

E. In what respect have I stated it differently?

Ch. I asked you expressly whether the lodge had anything to do with religion. You answered: "No, the lodge has nothing at all to do with religion."

E. I did say so. Is it not true?

Ch. No. You have a great deal to do with religion. You acknowledge, in religious matters, a highest "authority"; you have the Bible and use it, for you read the ten commandments and other portions of Scripture and apply them; you have Highpriests and Grand Highpriests, Chaplains, Grand Chaplains, and altars; you teach and confess the existence of a God, and demand faith in "a Supreme Being, the Ruler of the Universe"; you teach the duties we owe him, and lead men to obey his commandments; you teach the way to salvation, have your set prayers and religious ceremonies, for example, at funerals, dedication of lodges, and installation in the different degrees. All this is superfluous, if you have nothing to do with religion. That you have and make use of all this, is sufficient proof that you have much to do with religion. Indeed, I cannot consider you in any other light *than as a religious association.*

E. Yes, if you look at it in this light, and take everything so literally and exactly; but I cannot think that that has much to signify. When I said that we, as a lodge, had nothing to do with religion, I only meant that we do not rob any one of his faith, or compel him to accept another; and that we give no particular religious instruction, as, for instance, is given in a catechetical class. We do not baptize, we do not administer the communion, and just as little do we have a weekly sermon or religious discourse.

Ch. You do not compel any one, by external force, to accept your faith, and in so far can truly say that you let every one believe as he pleases. Yet, whoever wishes to be received, must confess that he believes in a divine being; for, should he deny that, you dare not accept him (Digest, page 361). Further, you have repeatedly said the lodge was nothing more than a benevolent and mutual aid association. To support and assist each other, that was its chief aim.

E. And is not that the chief aim of the lodge ?

Ch. No, it is not. See here, on page 47 ff. of the Manual, it is said: "The order, as founded by Brother Wildey, was simply a *humane* institution,—its *main* objects were to relieve brethren, bury the dead, and care for the widow and orphan. But gradually there were infused into its lectures and charges much moral and (unsectarian) *religious* instruction; and at each revision these principles were increased, and deepened, and strengthened, *until its beneficial and relief measures, from being ends, have become means to a higher and greater end*—"*to improve and elevate the character of man, to imbue him with con- conceptions of his capability for good, to enlighten his mind.*" On page 110 it says: "It is unfortunate for our order, and for not a few of its members, that too much prominence has been generally given to its feature of *pecuniary* benefits in seasons of sickness and death, and *pecuniary* aid in circumstances of want and distress. This, though a laudable and useful trait in our operations, *is hardly a tithe of our aims and objects.*" On page 117 we read: "Let no one unite with the order merely to . . . *insure himself provision* in case of sickness and distress." On page 261 it says: "It is time that those who unite with us . . . *but for the loaves and fishes*, should learn that *they have mistaken their aim.*" In the Pocket Companion, page 13, we read, that the order is *not* "a mere pecuniary advantage, as many unfortunately understand it to be." Many other passages which say the same thing, I could read to you, but think that these are sufficient to prove that your assertion, that mutual aid is the chief aim, is entirely false. There it stands, in clear and unmistakable terms, that "its beneficial and relief measures" are not "ends," but "*means to a higher and greater end.*" The lodge declares, in plain terms, "the pecuniary benefits" are "*hardly the tenth part of our aims and objects.*" It declares: "Let no one unite with the order" merely "*to insure pecuniary profits.*" Further, it declares that all who unite for this reason "*have missed their aim.*" The lodge therefore expresses, clearly and plainly, that it designs something higher and greater than pecuniary benefits.

E. I told you expressly, that we do not accept every one, but only moral, steady and religiously inclined persons Certainly we must care, besides for the benefits. for morality also. What would people think of us, if we suffered the members of the lodge to lead an immoral life?

Ch. The question is not, what sort of a life you lead, or should lead, according to the rules of your lodge, but that you have something to do with religion; indeed your religion is perhaps the chief end.

E. That this is the chief end, I cannot see. To be sure, when one considers the matter as you do, we have perhaps something to do with religion. I, however, look at it from a different point of view. Since we impart no particular religious instruction, do not baptize, do not administer the Lord's supper, allow every one to believe as he pleases, I say we have nothing to do with religion.

Ch. How can you talk like this? Pray, have the ten commandments, reading portions of the Scripture, religious discourses, the nominating, choosing and installing the High Priests and Chaplains, the religious ceremonies and prayers, nothing to do with religion?

E. The ten commandments and prayers certainly belong to religion.

Ch. You understand, therefore, that you have something to do with religion?

E. I grant that we have something of a *religious* nature, but nothing *sectarian*.

Ch. Whether you have anything sectarian or not, we will consider another time. You have, therefore, according to your own confession, something of religion, something to do with religion.* As Christians, we must now thoroughly prove whether this religion of yours coincides with the holy Scriptures.

E. Most assuredly it does, for do we not use the Scriptures? In them we are commanded to support the widows and orphans.

Ch. Well, we shall see. You believe, therefore, in one God, and demand faith in him, do you not?

E. Certainly.

Ch. What kind of a God is that in which you believe?

E. What a stupid question! In what kind of a God should we believe, than in the one true God, who has created the heavens and the earth, who preserves them, and who giveth us his rain and sunshine. I should think you might have known that.

Ch. Yes, but there are so many Gods, and we must be cautious that we do not mistake an idol for the true God! Is your God the Triune, that is, one Being and three Persons, or is he only one, that is, one Being and only one Person?

E. You know very well that the Bible, as well as our Catechism, teaches a Triune God, and he is our God as well as he is yours.

Ch. But you have Jews in your lodge, and Heathen and Turks may become members. Do they also believe in the Triune God?

E. I do not know, neither does it concern me in the least. I let every one believe what he pleases.

Ch. Have those Jews and Heathen who are received into the Lodge, answered the question, whether they believe in God, in the affirmative also?

---

* See Lodge Bulletin of July, 1871. There it says: "Oddfellowship has a morality, HAS A RELIGION, OR THEOLOGY."

E. Yes, certainly, else they would not have been received. In the subordinate lodge, of which I am a member, we have, however, no Heathen.

Ch. That may well be the case, that in your small lodge you have no Heathen or Mohammedans; but they might be accepted. See here, on page 238 of your Digest, it is said that it is not forbidden to propose any Infidel for membership, provided he believes "in a Supreme Being, the Creator and Preserver of the Universe," and that no unbelief disqualifies a man to become a member of the Order. The Pocket Companion expresses this yet more plainly on page 307, where it says: "Jew or Gentile, Catholic or Protestant, *is, as such,* welcome to our lodges." And the Manual, on page 374, coincides entirely therewith. Now, from this fact, that the Jews, Heathen and Mohammedans answer the question, whether they believe in God, in the affirmative, it follows with certainty that the lodge has not the Triune God; for the Jews do not believe in the Triune God, do not even receive the Old Testament as God's word, else they must become Christians. The Mohammedans, according to their Koran, believe in "Allah," but not in the Triune God, Father, Son and Holy Ghost, as he has revealed himself to us in the Holy Scriptures. Or can you imagine that a Heathen, Jew or Mohammedan, as soon as he becomes a member of the Lodge, believes in the Triune God of the Christians?

E. That is not very probable. If they have not been taught, they do not know him, and can therefore not believe in him; but it is our mission to instruct the weaker brethren.

Ch. And what is written in your books concerning God, proves quite clearly that the God which the lodge has, is not the Triune God.

E. Why, what do they say about him?

Ch. On page 114 of the Manual the God of the lodge is designated as "a Supreme Intellect, the Ruler of the Universe." On page 140 God is represented as the Father of all men, who, according to page 222, will make the members of the order "sharers of his immortality and eternal life." Whether they believe (in the biblical sense of the word) or not, makes no difference with this "universal Father" (page 366), according to the doctrines of the lodge. On page 388 we read: "Followers of different teachers, ye are worshipers of One God, who is Father of all, and *therefore ye are brethren.*" On page 387 it is said that "the three great religions of the world (Judaism, Christianity and Mohammedanism) recognize the One, only living and true God." The God of the lodge is, therefore, the "Supreme Intellect" (not a person), "the Ruler of the Universe," whom the Jews, Mohammedans and Christians recognize. That the Jews, however, have another God than the Triune, everybody knows, as well as that the Mohammedan believes in Allah, and not in the Father, Son and Holy Ghost. The lodge teaches that "followers of different teachers," let them be called Mohammed, Christ, Pope, Confucius, Voltaire, Paine or Luther, are "worshipers" of the same God. Indeed a dreadful lie, from which it is clear that the lodge has no other God than the God of Reason, that God which every one, by means of his reason, forms to himself; therefore an idol of his fancy, let him be Jew or Gentile, a Mohammedan or a Christian, who has denied the faith of the Bible.

E. There you go decidedly too far. When I say I believe in God, this my faith is not from reason, but from the Bible; therefore I do not believe in an idol of my own fancy, but in the true God; and I think the other brethren in the lodge do the same.

Ch. I am rejoiced to hear that you believe in the true God and not in an idol of reason; but the question here is not what *you* believe, neither what perhaps some other brethren of the lodge believe, but what the lodge teaches concerning God—what kind of a God it has. And that the lodge has only an idol of human reason, is proved most forcibly by the words I have just quoted, where it says the followers of different teachers are worshipers of the same God. Now, Mohammed was a teacher, and taught to worshig a being which he called Allah, which, however, never existed. The Pope claims to be a great teacher, and teaches the invocation, and therefore the adoration of the saints; for invocation is a way of praying. The Chinese follow their teachers, who instruct them to worship idols and slips of paper. The Fetish worshipers follow their teachers, who have taught them to worship shavings and potsherds. Our ancient Germans, while still heathen, followed their instructors when they worshiped springs, large oak trees, or the sun and moon. Can you now imagine that the worshipers of idols in China, the Fetish adorer, the snake worshiper, the adorer of Allah, and he who invokes the Saints, worship the *true* God?

E. Well, if they do not know him, they cannot worship him. But you consider the subject in a very wrong light. We hold fast to the main point, and that is, that there is a God. The lodge does not enter into a minute description of who or what God is. The main point is, there is a God, and the lodge holds fast to that.

Ch. I must decidedly deny that. What use, for example, to the worshiper of an idol, is the God which he imagines to dwell in his idol of wood or stone? Can this God save him? When he dies, can he grant him a peaceful end and receive him into Heaven? See: according to your opinion, the idolatrous heathen has the main point, viz., the belief that there is a God; and yet he lacks consolation, forgiveness of sins, life and salvation, and therefore everything. What good does *this* main point do him? About as much as *nothing*. And what a terrible insult it is to the majesty of our God, to imagine something else as God, to honor and worship it! That is to rob God the Lord of his honor! No, the main point is not the belief that there is a God. The main point is, that *we know the true God aright, and believe in him.* That is the main point.

E. Well, I told you it is our duty to instruct the weak brethren. If, then, some entertain wrong views concerning God, we can teach them better.

Ch. That must be a fine instruction indeed! When members of the lodge, which set up, recognize and defend this false doctrine, who have long ago rejected the doctrines of the Sacred Scriptures, or have never believed them,—when they give instruction concerning God, that must indeed be interesting. What kind of instruction, for instance, would it be, if a Mohammedan, a Jew or a worshiper of Nature would teach us about God, his Being and his Works? A fine instruction, indeed!

E. I believe, for certain, that what our books say about God, is entirely sufficient for the Lodge, and the more so because the people of Israel did not believe in the triune, but in the *one* God.

Ch. The question is not whether it is sufficient for the lodge or not, but whether what the lodge teaches of God coincides with the holy Scripture. And when you say that Israel did not believe in the Triune God, I cannot possibly agree with you. I can only say that the doctrine of the holy Trinity is not *so plainly and clearly revealed* in the Old as in the New Testament. That, however, this doctrine is contained in the Old Testament, and in the light of the New Testament becomes quite clear and evident, we see, for example, in the following passages: Gen. 1:1-3; Ps. 33:6; Numb. 6:24-26; Isaiah 48:16, 61, 1, 9, 3. Do we, then, find passages in the Old Testament from which it is evident that God is not *one*, but *three* persons? Then we have certainly no right to say Israel did not believe in the Triune God. If Israel believed in that God who revealed himself to them, and so far as he revealed himself to them, then they had the right, the true God. We, however, have not only the Old Testament, but also the New,—the complete Word of God; and in this word God has clearly and manifestly revealed himself as triune, that is, one Being and three Persons. (Compare Matt. 3:16, 17; John

14 : 16, 17; 2 Cor. 3 : 13.) Can you point me to one single passage in all the publications of your lodge which proves that the lodge believes in this Triune God, and requires faith in him from its members?

E. That I certainly cannot do. In all our writings, we speak only of God in general.

Ch. It is well that you give it up beforehand. You might seek to all eternity, but would not find any, for the simple reason that nothing of the kind stands in all your publications. If you, therefore, cannot even show one passage in all your Odd Fellow writings, can you still think that the lodge has the true Triune God, that it teaches and confesses him?

E. I do not really know how to answer you. I, for my part, believe in the Triune God, as I have learned in the school. What others believe, does not concern me. Every one has to answer for himself.

Ch. You do indeed seem to take it very easy, but the matter is a very serious one. Do you believe one can join a society which teaches false doctrine, without committing a great sin?

E. I do not know what wrong there would be in joining a society which makes material assistance its principal object, even when it does not agree in all points with our Lutheran doctrine. To aid and assist pecuniarily, that is our chief principle.

Ch. I entreat you, do not come again with your assertion that the lodge is exclusively, or even mainly, an association for mutual assistance. That is not true! See here, on page 110 of the Manual, the lodge declares that its pecuniary benefits are "hardly the tenth part" of its "ends and objects." On page 261 it is said that such as join the order for the sake of the benefits "have mistaken their aim." And on page 117 it is expressly said: "Let no one unite with the order merely to . . . secure himself assistance." It has, therefore, other aims than mutual aid. But what does the holy Scripture say about Christians uniting with heterodox bodies? Paul writes, 1 Tim. 5 : 22 : "Neither be partakers of other men's sins." That is done by joining a society which teaches and defends false doctrine, as the lodge certainly does; for thereby we consent to these false doctrines. acknowledge them, and assist such a society to disseminate them. And that is a great wrong. It is dreadful to approve and acknowledge the perversion of God's word. In this way we make God a liar, and ourselves tools to help other souls to be led into error and condemnation. It is a Christian's sacred duty to condemn every false doctrine, whenever he can; to protest against every perversion of God's word, and at all times to confess his Lord Jesus. If he neglect to do so, or even does the very contrary, he denies his Master, who has purchased him with such a great price. The Lord Jesus says: "Whosoever shall deny me before men, him will I also deny before my Father which is in heaven" (Matt. 10 : 33). And what position a Christian should maintain over against such bodies as teach false doctrine, St. Paul tells us in 2 Cor. 6 : 14–18 : "Be ye not unequally yoked together with unbelievers : for what fellowship hath righteousness with unrighteousness? And what communion hath light with darkness? And what concord hath Christ with Belial? Or what part hath he that believeth with an infidel? And what agreement hath the temple of God with idols? for ye are the temple of the living God; as God hath said, I will dwell in them and walk in them, and I will be their God, and they shall be my people. Therefore come out from among them and be ye separate, saith the Lord, and touch not the unclean thing." And in Eph. 5 : 11 the same Apostle says: "And have no fellowship with the unfruitful works of darkness, but rather reprove them." In the Epistle to the Galatians, chapter 1 : 8, 9, every one who teaches another gospel is even called accursed. As the word of God, then, is so much in earnest and so particular about it, I entreat you to do the same. However, the doctrine concerning God is not the only false doctrine of the lodge. It has more fundamental errors still.

E. Well, what next will you discover in our books? I am already said to deny the Lord; the lodge is said to teach fundamental errors; and who knows what next you bring up? But for to-day I have no more time to listen to your further objections; you must put them off till the next time. However, you must not exaggerate, must endeavor to look upon every subject in the best possible light, and to speak good of it as far as ever you can.

Ch. Well, if you have no time, I will not detain you longer. Only come soon again, that we may converse more about the matter. We must necessarily examine it carefully.

E. Certainly I hope, too, you will gain a better opinion of our order when you first come to know how much good it has already accomplished.

Ch. Very well; our further discussion will show.

FOURTH DIALOGUE.

> Not by works of righteousness which we have done, but according to his mercy, he saved us, by the washing of regeneration and renewing of the Holy Ghost. Titus 3 : 5.

Ernest. Well, dear neighbor, I am most anxious to hear what further false doctrines or fundamental errors the lodge entertains. Since our last conversation I have thought a great deal what kind of false doctrines they might be. I must, however, honestly confess I have not been able to discover them. I then thought you must be a real hypochondriac, who suspects nothing but ghosts, dreadful spectres, and all kinds of monsters, when only a small cloud passes over. The recollection of your dream confirms me in this opinion.

Christian. I would willingly bear the name of a hypochondriac, if by this means the lodge could be purified from its really fundamental errors; but that, alas! is impossible. The false doctrines of the lodge are evident; and they are not lessened in the least, even if the lodge calls me and other Christians who cannot approve them, hypochondriacs. The more I think of it, the more it horrifies me, especially because so many weak Christian souls, unsuspicious of evil, are drawn into the lodge, and gradually become so blinded that they do not perceive these false doctrines; yea, even consider them to be true, and so are in the greatest danger of losing their souls.

E. Well, really, that promises to get interesting. You are perhaps ready to condemn all the Odd Fellows.

Ch. God be praised, I am far from it. On the contrary, I love the Odd Fellows, and would gladly do them all manner of good; but their false doctrines I must condemn; or rather not I, but the word of God condemns them.

E. Which are, then, these frightful errors? I am anxious to hear them.

Ch. Very well; for to-day we will hear but one.

E. Which one?

Ch. Tell me, how can we be saved?

E I think you ought to know that. The Bible says, Repent and believe in the Lord Jesus Christ.

Ch. Quite correct. I rejoice to hear that you have not got so far as many lodge members, who would be saved by their own works. But does the lodge teach this way of salvation? No, by no means. Before any one can repent, he must be brought by the law of God to a knowledge of his sins. He must know that he has many times transgressed all the commandments of his God, and thereby offended the holy and just God, provoked his wrath and indignation, and deserves death and eternal damnation. He must know that it is literally true, when our Catechism, in the Second Article, calls every man a lost and condemned sinner, as well on account of original as for actual sin. Does the lodge strive to produce and to awaken this knowledge in its members?

E. I do not know that they have that in view, and consider it to be quite superfluous. The Bible teaches the way of salvation, and it is a clergyman's duty to explain it to us: so the lodge surely need not do it.

Ch. Certainly it need not, as it is not called to do so. Nevertheless, it does teach a way to salvation, and this is a dreadful heresy, that it teaches *another* way to salvation than the holy

Scriptures do, and thereby leads all who imbibe the poison of this false doctrine in the way to destruction. In all your publications, not a single passage occurs acknowledging that all men by nature are under the curse of original sin; no passage showing that "the thoughts and imaginations of the human heart are evil continually"; no passage teaching that "out of the heart proceed evil thoughts, murders, adulteries, fornications, thefts, false witness, blasphemies" (Matt. 15 : 19 ;—no single passage from which we could conclude that the lodge acknowledges that every one is accursed, and under the everlasting wrath of God, "that continueth not in all things which are written in the book of the law to do them" (Gal. 8 : 10.)

E. It is, however, more than once said in them, that all men have their faults, and surely faults are sins.

Ch. To be sure that is said in them. But can you show me a passage in which the faults are set down as sins against the holy and just God, and subject men to his wrath and punishment; one passage in which it is said that we by such faults deserve everlasting condemnation ?

E. It is true, it is not considered such a serious matter.

Ch. The lodge knows nothing at all about God's wrath over sin. To help its members to a knowledge of their sins ; to prove them to be poor sinners, is not at all its object. On the contrary, it uses all endeavors to stifle the sense and consciousness of sin in its members, by continually extolling its members and their deeds, and tries to make every man believe *he is capable of doing good.* On page 47 ff. of the Manual it says that the lodge recognizes its mission to be "to improve and elevate the character of man ; to imbue him with conceptions of *his capability for good.* From page 112 ff. we learn "*the most important uses and aims*" of Oddfellowship to be "*the imbuing of the minds of our brethren with proper conceptions of their powers and capacities.*" The praise of the lodge and its deeds is found upon almost every page of your writings. In the Manual, page 69, it is said, for example, : "What institution .... has accomplished more good and prevented more suffering in so few years?" On page 68 it is said, the order has "driven back the waves of ignorance, vice and selfishness everywhere, and has moulded into a kindred likeness of benevolence, not a few institutions nearly as powerful for good as itself." On page 72 we read: "The name of Odd Fellow has been rendered dear to our hearts *by the glorious deeds of benevolence and philanthropy* performed under it." And so the praise is sounded continually through all your writings; one can scarcely read a page or two in all your journals without stumbling over such detestable self-praise. All these periodicals are almost nothing else than compilations of lamentable self-exaltation, which serves to blind the members more and more, to awaken and nourish the feeling of imaginary greatness; and on the contrary, gradually to stifle the feeling of one's own sinfulness entirely. But self-praise is no recommendation.

E. But we are commanded to do good works, and as our order does many excellent ones, I do not think it is wrong to publish them.

Ch. To be sure, a Christian does good works. But I beg you, let us treat of that another time, and, for to-day, stick to the question, How can we be saved? The first step to it is the confession of our sins, as well as the knowledge that we have thereby deserved God's wrath and punishment. Furthermore, true repentance and sorrow for sin is also required. As the lodge, however, knows nothing of sin, nor of the anger of the holy and just God against sin, it also knows nothing of repentance and sorrow for sin. It is entirely ignorant of that repentance which needeth not to be repented of. Indeed it must seem eminently ridiculous to a brother of your lodge, that a David should water his couch with tears of repentance, or that Manasseh should weep for his sins, as also Peter. Your answer, a while ago, was quite correct, that we could only be saved by repentance and faith. Now it must be clear to you that the lodge neither teaches nor does anything that might lead any one to the knowledge of sin; is entirely ignorant of, and does not care about repentance before God for our manifold sins. As it therefore knows nothing about sin (in the biblical sense of the word), knows and cares nothing about repentance and sorrow before God, it, of course, knows nothing of *faith in Jesus Christ, the Savior of sinners, nothing of the forgiveness of sins.* Indeed the lodge, according to the position it has assumed, can neither know nor care anything about these things.

E. Pray, *why* can it know nothing about these things?

Ch. Tell me, do you look for a physician when you are not sick?

E Certainly not.

Ch. Well, the lodge is not sick from the wounds of sin; it considers itself quite well; therefore it seeks no physician, indeed will not have one. You know, however, that our Lord Jesus Christ, true God and true man, is the physician of suffering souls. Does the lodge acknowledge Jesus Christ to be true God? Please show me one single passage in all these Odd Fellow publications, where Jesus Christ is recognized as the true God. Do show me one!

E. At this moment I certainly cannot do so, but I think surely there are some to be found.

Ch. No, dear neighbor, there is not a single one in them all. Neither can there be any, on account of the Jews whom you have in your lodge, on account of the Heathen and Turks* whom you have taken in, and to whom the door of the lodge stands open; for they would not suffer it. It denies, therefore, at least tacitly,

---

* See Pocket Comp., page 128, fl. 306, 309. Manual, p. 383. Digest, p. 238.

that God the Father so loved the world that he gave his only begotten son (John 3 : 16). It denies that Jesus Christ is "the true God, and eternal life" (1 John 5 : 20). It denies that Jesus Christ "came, who is over all, God, blessed forever" (Rom. 9 : 5). It denies that "God is revealed in the flesh" (1 Tim. 3 : 16). That it is God's will "that all men should honor the Son, even as they honor the Father" (John 5 : 23). What do you think, however? Is it a chief and fundamental doctrine of our Christianity, that Jesus Christ is the Son of God, or is it only an unimportant, insignificant doctrine?

E. Most assuredly it is a fundamental doctrine of our Christianity.

Ch. Certainly it is. With it Christianity stands or falls. If Jesus Christ is not the Son of God, the whole plan of redemption is nothing; we are, then, still in our sins; cannot through eternity be saved; indeed the entire holy Scripture is then nothing but a book of intense deception. And this fundamental article of the Christian faith the lodge rejects; it therefore robs every one who believes its teachings of the foundation of his faith, the foundation of his salvation in time and in eternity. To warn us against such enemies of our faith, John writes, in his first Epistle, chap. 4 : 3 : "And every spirit that confesseth not that Jesus Christ is come in the flesh, is not of God"; and admonishes us (2 John, v. 10) not to receive such. However, he says, in John 4 : 15 : "Whosoever shall confess that Jesus is the Son of God, God dwelleth in him, and he in God."

E. I do not remember a single passage in our books where it is said Jesus Christ is not the Son of God; on the contrary, he is often referred to as to a wise man, and his example is sometimes recommended in the Manual for imitation.

Ch. That is just the trouble, that the lodge does not use plain and honest language when it speaks of the subject. It does not believe that Jesus Christ is the Son of God, and yet it does not say so in plain terms, that simple, weak Christians can readily understand it. It is not, however, without design that it thus plays at hide and seek. Should it declare, in round terms, "We do not believe that Jesus is the Son of God," and should it make this publicly known, how many of those who still value in some degree their Christianity, would it gain? Would you have joined it if it had made such a declaration?

E. By no means would I have done so.

Ch. The gentlemen of the Grand Lodge of the United States, who are at the helm, and who have all the other Odd Fellows in leading-strings, know this very well, and therefore endeavor to give themselves a Christian appearance before Christians. We have the Bible and read in it, they say; yea, they even declare, "We believe the Bible," merely to catch such souls as still love God's word. We need not wonder at this serpent-like cunning, for the Devil, the father of lies, acts just so. He transforms himself, as Paul says (2 Cor. 11 : 14), "into an angel of light." That was his way not only with Adam and Eve in Paradise; he is the same to this day. The lodge, however, rejects not only the fundamental doctrine that Jesus is the Son of God, but also the other important and essential truth, that we, through nothing else than Jesus' blood and wounds, obtain grace, forgiveness, life and salvation. You said, a while ago, that your books sometimes refer you to the example of Jesus; but that cannot save us. Can you now prove from your books that you, with all your "faults," are directed to the blood of Christ in order to seek forgiveness there?

E. It is true, I never read that in them.

Ch. I believe that, for there is nothing said of that in them. Now, the holy Scripture teaches: 'Neither is there salvation in any other" than in Jesus Christ (Acts 4 : 12). It teaches: "The blood of Jesus Christ, his Son, cleanseth us from all sin" (1 John 1 : 7). It teaches: "In whom (Christ) we have redemption through his blood, the forgiveness of sins" (Eph. 1 : 7). The lodge, however, denies all this, and rejects the forgiveness of sins through the blood of Christ. The Scripture teaches, further, that Christ was made a curse for us (Gal. 3 : 13); was made sin for us (2 Cor. 5 : 21); our sins and iniquities were laid upon him (Isa. 53), that he might bear them and gain forgiveness for us. And whoever asks, What shall I do to be saved? is pointed to him with the words, "Believe in the Lord Jesus Christ and thou shalt be saved and thy house" (Acts 16 : 30, 31), or with the words, "Repent and believe the gospel" (Mark 1 : 15). For faith in Christ alone it is by which we can be justified before God, as it is so clearly and distinctly taught in the sacred Scriptures. Paul writes (Rom. 3 : 28): "Therefore we conclude that a man is justified by faith, without the deeds of the law;" and (Rom. 10 : 4): "For Christ is the end of the law for righteousness to every one that believeth." And the Lord Jesus says that "whosoever believeth in the Son of God shall not perish, but have everlasting life" (John 3 : 16). This, however, the lodge rejects likewise, and does not believe in salvation by grace through the merits of Jesus Christ. The lodge does not, like John the Baptist, point the poor sinner to Christ and say: "Behold the Lamb of God, which taketh away the sin of the world" (John 1 : 29). No, it does the very contrary, and endeavors to keep every one away from Christ.

E. You should not pick so at everything. You seem to be a real hair-splitter. Consider how much good the order has already accomplished and is continually doing, and remember that on earth nothing is perfect.

Ch. Well, you must first remember that we cannot be too careful and particular with what God tells us in his pure word. And in this matter I am not at all displeased if you call me a hair-splitter. I also promise you to consider and properly regard whatever good the order has. And, as you seem to take that so much at heart, let us in our next conversation take that for our subject.

E. I am rejoiced to hear that, and can tell you that I shall be ready for you.

Ch. Very good. But to-day I have to prove to you yet that the lodge teaches a way to salvation. That the lodge don't want to know anything of repentance and faith, and of Jesus Christ as our Redeemer and Savior. and therefore of the true way to salvation, you must see and acknowledge, if you will be honest. What kind of a way to salvation does it, then, teach? It teaches, like the real Pharisees and the Pope, a way of salvation *by so-called good works.* And this is so frequently and repeatedly expressed, that it is as clear as daylight, and not the least doubt remaining. I have, a while ago, quoted from the Manual (page 47, 113) that the lodge declares it to be its *chief aim* to imbue the minds of the brethren with proper conceptions of their powers and capabilities, and to inculcate the idea that they are capable of *doing good.* It teaches, therefore, that man is of himself capable of doing good. What, however, is the teaching of the sacred Scripture? It says (Rom. 3 : 12): "They are all gone out of the way; they are together become unprofitable; there is none that doeth good, no, not one." In the second Epistle to the Corinthians, chap. 3, the same man of God says that we are not even capable of *thinking anything good*, as of ourselves. And the reason for this is, because we are conceived and born in sin (Ps. 51); because the thoughts and imaginations of the heart of man are evil from his youth, and continually (Gen. 6 : 8); and because out of the heart proceed evil thoughts, all sins and abominations (Matt. 15 : 19). If, now, the source, namely, the heart, be evil, how can the actions be good which spring from a corrupt and depraved source? The lodge, however, in direct contradiction to the word of God, teaches: Man of himself is capable of doing good. And further: whoever, as a genuine Odd Fellow, does good; that is, whoever pays his fees when due, watches, as is his duty, with the sick when his turn comes, guards against grave offences, and endeavors to lead a respectable life,— he shall be saved. It would require hours, should I read you all the passages that teach this doctrine. To prove it, I will adduce but a few. In the Pocket Companion, on page 27, it is said: "They (the doctrines of the lodge) lead him to obedience of the commandments of his Divine Maker, in which HE CANNOT FAIL to be blessed in life, death and eternity." On page 41 ff. we read: "He who practices this charity, and teaches it to others, shall be crowned with honor, and come down to the grave in peace, *with the full assurance of a blessed future.*" He can then, according page 138, "*come up through it with joy and gladness to the land of eternal light,*" and meets, according to page 182, "with an eternal welcome in that 'angel land,' and there rests, reclining his head "on the satisfactory pillow of contentment." In the Manual, page 157, it is said : "With 'a conscience void of offence toward God and man,' he lives, . . . *and his departure from earth is but a translation to a blissful immortality.*" Here, in clear and unmistakable terms, it is said that every Odd Fellow who comes up to his duties will be saved, let him have a sense of his sinfulness or not, let him repent or not, let him believe in Christ or not. About this the lodge does not concern itself, if he only is and remains a good Odd Fellow, does not withdraw from the lodge (for by doing so he is, according to the declaration of the lodge, "dead"); if he faithfully pays his fees, and is obedient to the lodge in all things; then he will be saved. The lodge therefore teaches a salvation, not through Christ, but without Christ; not by the means of grace, the word of God and the holy Sacraments, but without these; not by repentance and faith, but without repentance and faith. It therefore denies the only true way to salvation, and teaches a false way. It pretends to teach the way to heaven, but really teaches the way to hell; pretends to be a guide to the kingdom of heaven, and leads straight down to everlasting destruction. Oh, I shudder when I think of it, that through this satanic doctrine so many weak Christian souls are led astray, and, if they continue in these fundamental heresies, must finally be lost to all eternity. What a dreadful sentence will, on the judgment day be pronounced against the lodge which thus tramples the word of God under foot, which for itself bars the way to Heaven by such false teachings, and restlessly works night and day to draw more souls into its net. The word of God leaves us no merit as regards our salvation, and teaches that we can be saved alone by grace. We read, for example (Tit. 3 : 5): "*Not by works of righteousness which we have done, but according to his mercy he saved us.*" In Eph. 2 : 8, 9, it says: "*For by grace are ye saved through faith; and that not of yourselves, it is the gift of God. Not of works, lest any man should boast.*" In Gal. 2 : 16, says the Apostle: "Knowing that a man is not justified by the works of the law, but by the faith of Jesus Christ." In John 8 : 36 it is written: "He that *believeth* on the Son, *hath everlasting life.*" In these and similar texts, all our own merit is cut off, and we are *alone* pointed to the grace of God in Christ, to his bloody merits, sufferings and death. And only to him who, by faith, apprehends this truth, and remains faithful to the end, so that he can say with Paul (2 Tim 4 : 7, 8), "I have kept the faith," to him, *through grace*, shall the crown of everlasting life be given. But, as your lodge teaches the direct opposite of this way to salvation, and therefore preaches another gospel, the dreadful words which you will find in Gal. 1 : 8, 9, will apply to it also. I entreat you to read and reflect on them before it is too late.

FIFTH DIALOGUE.

> So likewise ye, when ye shall have done all things which are commanded you, say, We are unprofitable servants: we have done that which was our duty to do. Luke 17 : 10.

Ernest. This time we shall treat of the benevolence of our order, shall we not?

Christian. Yes, sir.

E. I am very glad of it, for now I can, for once, put in a word. The last time, you had it nearly all to yourself.

Ch. I will gladly let you say all you have to say, only I entreat you to speak of good works in the sense of the holy Scriptures.

E. That I intend to do.

Ch. Then please communicate to me, in a clear and thorough manner, your good works, your deeds of benevolence and charity.

E. Gladly. I have informed you repeatedly that our order is a society whose object is mutual aid and benevolence, and has already been the means of doing much good, and is continually doing so. Therefore it is most desirable that every one should join it, in order that the necessary means may be increased, and the order extend its benefits farther and farther; yes, gradually encircle the earth in Friendship, Love and Truth. I hope now to convince you that these are not mere empty words, but facts.— In the first place, that is no insignificant benefit, that, when I am ill, I receive regularly three or five dollars every week during my whole sickness; upon which sum a family, that is not over large, can comfortably subsist for a period, if they exercise a little economy. So, also, it is not lightly to be esteemed, that during my illness, if necessary, or if I desire it, every night two brothers watch by my bedside to nurse me, and with pleasure procure for me every possible alleviation of my sufferings. And, to have these night-watchers, my wife need not run from house to house to beg people to come, nor to pay these watchers a high price, as is so frequently the case; no, the lodge provides them of its own accord, so soon as I have reported myself sick, or any of the brothers have found it out. Should I die, my wife need not worry where to get the necessary funds to defray the funeral expenses; the lodge sends her the thirty or fifty dollars to the house. Indeed, if she finds it too hard to make the arrangements for the funeral, the lodge with great readiness, regarding it as a charitable act, does it for her, and in a solemn and honorable way.—In the second place, it is an incalculable benefit, that the widow, according to her necessities, receives regularly her monthly assistance, so that she can look into the dark future without care for sustenance. Oh, how many a widow, after her husband's death, has had to battle with the most terrible cares! How many struggle almost desperately for the daily morsel for themselves and their poor children! How many have been driven by their necessities, in despair, to murder their children and to commit suicide! How many a poor widow is, besides, oppressed and robbed by merciless wretches, because she has no protector! Ah, all this none of our widows has to fear. The lodge provides for them, protects and helps them.—Then it is another great benefit, that the lodge provides for the orphans' temporal and spiritual wants Should, for example, the mother not be able or willing to educate the children, the lodge, at her desire, takes their education into its own hands, sends them to proper schools and academies, and sees that they are well taught and trained —Before I became a member of the lodge, I used to think, with great anxiety of mind, of my perhaps speedy death, because I was then unable to leave enough for the support of my dear family. But now, let me die when I may, I have no further anxiety on this score, for I know that they are provided for. You cannot believe what tranquillity it affords one to know his family is provided for. Yes, I could almost say, I thank God that I have learned to know the lodge and become a member of it.

But the benefactions and charitable deeds of our order extend farther. We are brothers, have devoted our lives to the brotherhood, and solemnly promised to stand by and assist each other where we possibly can. We derive great advantages therefrom. For example, if I wish to purchase anything, I go to a brother, and I know he will not cheat me, and will give me the goods as cheap as he can afford. If one is a laborer or mechanic, he can depend upon it, in case there are many lodge members in the place, that he will obtain work sooner, have more of it, and be better paid for it, if he belong to the lodge, than if he be not a member. And the beauty of it is, that our order extends far and near, not only over the United States, but also to Canada, Australia, Germany and Switzerland. And in other countries a commencement to introduce it has already been made. Thus, if a member finds no work in our State and goes to another, the brothers are immediately at hand to assist him and to procure work for him. If any one is on a journey and becomes sick, he is never forsaken; in every place he finds brothers who are ready to help him. But we do not only support the members of our order; no, we assist others likewise. Our order has expended considerable sums on such that suffered want or misfortune and who were not members; has supported many widows and orphans both in and outside of the order. But, as figures are said not to lie, I will furnish you some. Our order supported, for **example**, from June, 1867, until June, 1868, 21,344 members and 3,911 families. The members received $458,538.28; the families, $113,275.01; for the education of orphans, $19,957 were expended, and for the funerals of deceased brothers the sum of $103,847.50. The total amount of aid was $695,618.26, whilst the receipts for the same period reached the sum of $2,110,951.66. In the second following year, which ended with the 30th of June, 1870, 25,019 brothers were aided with $579,043.81, and 3,876 families of widows with $122,043.65; the orphans' fund received $19,444.16; the funeral expenses amounted to $132,659.21. Total amount for aid was $859,906.86; total amount of receipts, $2,724,419.46. For 1872, the amount paid for aid was $1,503,471.40; whereas the income amounted to $4,291,071.72. There was, therefore, a surplus of $2,787,599.72.* Well, I think these figures speak for themselves. I would like to know if you can name a similar association that accomplishes as much good as our order; but you will probably be unable to find one. However, you would be greatly mistaken, if you thought these were the only advantages offered by the lodge. No; the advantages and blessings are not merely of a material, but also of a spiritual nature. The lodge aims at the cultivation and perfection of its members both mentally and morally; its lessons and admonitions show how we should live, as virtuous citizens, among our fellow-men; yea, it teaches us not only our duty toward our fellow-men, but also better to know and fulfill our duties to God, as you will have seen in our books. The intellectual horizon of the members is enlarged, their minds improved; superstition vanishes more and more; indeed the mind is directed to entirely new objects. Besides, hundreds, yes thousands, by joining the lodge, are kept from bad company, from frequenting drinking saloons, from gambling,

---

* See Proceedings of Annual Communication of the Grand Lodge of the United States, of 1870, page 4779; and 1873, page 5666.

drinking, &c. I could cite much more to show you the benefits and charities of the order, and its blessed effects at home and abroad. But to be brief, the Order of Odd Fellows is one of the most benevolent associations, in material as well as spiritual, in temporal as well as moral results, which exists upon earth, and I hope this brief account will have convinced you of this fact.

Ch. We must now necessarily consider the boasted "benefits," "good works" and "charitable deeds" one by one, and examine them strictly; for "all is not gold that glitters." All this is, however, nothing new to me, for I know it all from your writings. In the first place, I would refer to an expression which you made use of toward the close of your panegyric, namely, that the order teaches also duties toward God. I am surprised that you still reckon this among the good works, as you, as a Christian, must now well know that it is a Satanic work, because the lodge knows only an idol of human reason, and therefore is guilty of idolatry every time it teaches the knowledge of him, and seeks to lead others into idolatry every time it demands the fulfillment of duties toward this idol. You remarked, very truly, that the mind of the lodge members is turned into an entirely different direction. The Christian's mind is turned to the Lord Jesus, to faith in him. He loves his Savior, who has first loved him, and seeks obediently to follow him. This turn of mind, gradually and almost unobservedly, receives another direction, after uniting with the lodge. For his Lord Jesus, the Savior of sinners, he suffers an "example" to be substituted; in the place of the living God, an idol of human reason. While formerly his faith clung to and received God's word with humility, smart and refined reason now assumes the place of God's word and of living faith, and he begins to pass judgment upon and to criticise God's word, its preaching, and the holy Sacraments. And it usually does not take long before he begins to consider himself highly enlightened, becomes indifferent to the Word and Sacraments; indeed he soon learns to despise them. It is not "superstition" that vanishes with the lodge members, but *faith*, and infidelity steps into its place. That this is true, experience proves. I need only ask you, upon your conscience, whether it is not your experience, that true faith, sincere love for the preaching of the divine word and for the sacraments, generally die away when one unites with the lodge, and I am convinced you must answer "Yes." This is the reason why one so rarely meets with a Free Mason or Odd Fellow who really *loves* the preaching of repentance and faith, and who holds the church dearer than the lodge. The experience, alas! is quite common, that the members hold the lodge dearer than the church, with her pure word and sacraments, with her preaching of repentance and faith, of forgiveness of sins, life and salvation. Did not the editor of "Heart and Hand" declare, in the number of July 22d, 1871, that he would much rather leave the church than the lodge? Is not this truly frightful! That you, having been more than ten years connected with the lodge, still stand as you do, cling to the church and the word of God, is a wonder of God's grace, a very rare exception, for which we ought to heartily thank God.—But let us now look at the benefactions singly and more closely. You said that members in sickness receive their weekly aid. Where does the lodge get the money which it pays in cases of sickness?

E. Why, every member must pay his fixed contribution every week.

Ch. And for that he receives the assistance in case of sickness?

E. Yes, sir.

Ch. Well, then no sensible man can call that a benefaction, yea, even a deed of charity or a good work. That is nothing more than a mutual contract: A member pays weekly so and so much, and when he is sick, receives therefor so and so much. It would certainly never come into any one's mind to call that a good work, when two, three or more persons enter into partnership to engage in business, and every one pays a certain sum, and shares in the profits of the concern according to the payment he made. Would the company, when they pay one his share of the profits, say to him, See what a benefit we confer upon you by giving you so much money? Certainly not. It is therefore ridiculous when the lodge boasts of its benefactions and charities, where it has indeed done no deed of charity, but simply come up to the obligations of its contract.

E. But it is a benefit for me, when I, in case of sickness, receive aid.

Ch. If it is a benefit for you, you have to thank yourself, and not the lodge, for it; for, had you paid nothing, you would have received nothing.

E. But had the lodge not existed, I could not have paid, and therefore could not have received anything, and in so far, I must consider it a benefit, and am grateful to the lodge for it.

Ch. For that it needs no lodge, with its false teachings and secret dealings. If one must absolutely belong to a society, there are other societies enough, such as societies for assistance in sickness, laborers' unions, and so forth. How you can consider yourself indebted to the lodge, I cannot comprehend. I might with as good reason say, the lodge is indebted to you, because you have contributed to it. Indeed it is really ludicrous, that you make such an absurd boasting of your benevolence, your deeds of charity and good works; and it is nothing but pitiful braggadocio, by which you want to catch the foolish and to induce them to join. What has become, then, of your motto, "Truth"? I see nothing but falsehood.

E. If you will not let our mutual aid pass as deeds of benevolence and charity, you must certainly acknowledge what the lodge does for widows and orphans as such. The lodge has entered into no obligation with me to give my wife, after my death, a certain sum monthly, and yet it does so, if there is need of it. Still less has contraticted to provide for and to educate my children, and yet it does so if necessary. All this it does for hundreds and thousands of widows and orphans, from pure love.

Ch. I cannot say that that is a work of love.

E. Well, you really must be struck with blindness, if you cannot see that!

Ch. Yes, sir, I am a peculiar man, who cannot declare anything to be a good work or deed of charity, unless the Scripture declares it to be such.

E. Well, neither would I declare any other to be good. But the Scripture says expressly that that is pure religion, when one cares for the widows and orphans.

Ch. We must first gain a clear idea of what the Scriptures call a good work or deed of charity. Tell me, what is a good work?

E. Why, when, for example, we give to a poor person bread, provisions or money.

Ch. Is that then a good work, if somebody, from whatever motive, gives a poor man ten dollars?

E. Certainly, that is a good work.

Ch. Tell me, then, why do you contribute that the widows and orphans of the brotherhood may be helped?

E. Because it is my duty as a Christian, because the widows and orphans need it, and because it will be very pleasant for my own family to receive aid, should they stand in need of it.

Ch. Would you contribute to the support of the widows and orphans of the members of the lodge, if you had no hope that your own family, in case of need, would be supported after your death?

E. I must honestly confess that in that case I would not contribute. I would invest my savings in some other way, that my family could have the benefit of them after my death.

Ch. Therefore you give to the lodge that you may receive it again; give something to the widows and orphans, that your own may receive something, if they should need it. Is it not so?

E. Certainly.

Ch. Do you believe that giving thus is a good work?

E. I think so. It certainly comes good to the widows and orphans, and benefits them, if they receive so and so much a month.

Ch. The question here is not, whether it benefits them, but whether it is a good work, and such a one as God himself declares in his word to be good, and has promised to reward in Heaven. Hear what the Lord Jesus says (Luke 6 : 33–35) : "And if ye do good to them which do good to you, what thank have ye? for sinners also do even the same. And if ye lend to them of whom ye hope to receive, what thank have ye? for sinners also lend to sinners, to receive as much again. But love ye your enemies, and do good and lend, hoping for nothing again; and your reward shall be great, and ye shall be the children of the Highest." In the time of Christ there were also such, who lent and gave because they hoped to receive it again. And now the Lord Jesus says, if ye give, hoping to receive again, what thank have ye? The publicans and gross sinners do the same; you have your reward. Exactly the same you do in your lodge: you give in order to receive again, and then boast of it as of a good work. The Lord Jesus, however, places you, in this respect, on a level with the publicans and such as live in open sin. Experience teaches the truth of what the Lord says; for one great sinner helps the other. It would certainly be difficult to find a thief who would not assist his thievish companions, in the hope of receiving aid from them at some other time. You do not give out of love to those that are widows and orphans, but (strictly speaking) only from love to your own family, from love to your own flesh and blood. Surely it cannot be difficult for you to perceive, that to pay **your** money in order to receive again, is not a good work.

E. Well, these are queer views! You place us on a level with thieves and robbers; indeed you will end by declaring us all to be thieves.

Ch. I do not declare you to be thieves. When you, however, assert that these your payments are good works, the Lord Jesus places your so-called good works in the same category with the good works of sinners and publicans, who, in their manner, do exactly the same.

E. I would really like to know what you consider to be good works. You will, perhaps, not even consider that a good work when the lodge, for instance, in public calamities, such as devastations through fire or water, assists the sufferers who do not belong to the lodge, and does so, often very liberally and in large sums, for which it certainly does not receive anything in return.

Ch. Even that, according to the Holy Scriptures, I cannot declare to be a good work.

E. Why not?

Ch. Because the Holy Scripture declares (Rom. 14 : 23): "Whatsoever is not of faith is sin." The assistance to the sufferers which the lodge perhaps now and then bestows, cannot spring from faith in Jesus Christ, because it neither has nor wants to have Jesus, but rejects him and does not believe in him. All your much vaunted good works proceed from unbelief, and therefore, in the sight of God, are nothing but sin.

E. Do you really think that those who do not believe in Christ, are incapable of doing good works?

Ch. No unbeliever can perform such works as God recognizes to be good and rewards in Heaven. He may perform works which the world calls good, extols and praises; but with these we have nothing to do. To perform works which are recognized by God and rewarded in Heaven, is impossible to an unbeliever, simply because he does not believe in Christ.

E. How will you prove that?

Ch. Simply by the holy Scriptures. I have just quoted what the Apostle says,—"Whatsoever is not of faith is sin." Therefore, as the works of an unbeliever and the works of the Lodge do not spring from faith in Christ Jesus, they are sinful. The Lord Jesus says (John 15 : 5): "Without me ye can do nothing." Therefore, as the lodge performs all its works without Christ, we can accordingly pronounce them to be lost, unprofitable, yea, corrupt and rotten works. What do you think? Can we procure good drinking water from a foul spring or a mud puddle?

E. No, certainly not.

Ch. Now, behold! our hearts, by nature, are just such foul springs; all evil, at least in its germ, dwells in them, because we are corrupt through sin. From this evil source no good work can proceed, until the Lord Jesus by his word and spirit has converted this evil source into a good one. This, however, only takes place when he brings us to true repentance and conversion, grants us forgiveness of our sins, renews and changes us so that we are enabled to say: "Old things have passed away, all things have become new." In this manner the Holy Spirit makes us capable of performing good works, that is, works which are done in and through faith in Christ Jesus, to which we are constrained from ardent love to him, who has first loved us; which serve to honor God and to benefit our neighbor, and whereby we would fain show the gratitude we owe to God. Such truly believing Christians give to the poor, not to receive again, but because they love Christ and in Christ the poor brethren, as redeemed children of God and heirs of salvation. Such Christians feed the hungry, give drink to the thirsty, clothe the naked, give to the poor, help the widows and orphans, bury the dead, not that the same may be done to them, but from grateful love to Christ. They experience daily how much good the Lord Jesus bestows upon them out of pure love; they would fain show their gratitude to him for this love by doing good to his members. To such Christians the Lord will say, on the judgment day: "I was an hungered and ye gave me meat; I was thirsty and ye gave me drink: I was a stranger and ye took me in, naked and ye clothed me; I was sick and ye visited me; I was in prison and ye came unto me." "Inasmuch as ye have done it unto one of the least of these my brethren, ye have done it unto me" (Matt. 25). The Lord Jesus himself must first make us fit and capable of doing good works, as is clearly taught in the Scriptures; for example, Eph. 2:19, Tit. 2:14, Heb. 18:21. The lodge, however, will not suffer Jesus Christ to make it fit and capable to do them; therefore it is impossible that it should perform good works. Would you assert that the lodge, for Christ's sake, from love to him, aids and assists anybody?

E. I really do not know what to answer you; but this I do know, that the Christian congregations do not relieve distress as they should do. And for this reason I think we should gratefully acknowledge it when the lodge takes hold and helps to mitigate suffering.

Ch. You are afraid to approach the matter, as a cat is afraid to touch the hot porridge. Pray stick to the point. First answer my question, whether you believe the lodge aids and assists anybody for Christ's sake. Afterward we may, for all I care, consider in how far the Christian congregations come up to their duties. Do you, then, believe that the lodge gives aid for Christ's sake?

E. Well, I could not very well assert that; neither can we say that of any other aid or insurance society.

Ch. Very well. If you concede, therefore, that the lodge does not help for Christ's sake, then you must also concede that in doing so it does no good works; that your boasting about good works is falsehood, and contrary to the Word of God, and is only done to throw sand into other people's eyes. Indeed, if you will be honest, you must also concede that your charities must displease God, because they proceed from unbelief, and only *serve selfish purposes.* In respect to other aid and insurance associations, I would only observe, that they come under the same condemnation, so soon as they boast of their works as good works which will take them to Heaven. But let us look a little closer at your charities. It is true, you have expended a considerable sum for charitable purposes. How many brothers did you say were supported during the year ending with the 30th of June, 1870?

E. During that year, 25,091 brothers received $579,043.81.

Ch. Were all of them in need of assistance, indigent, or suffering want?

E. That I do not know. With us, every one receives assistance so soon as he is sick, let him be rich or poor. Every one pays alike and every one receives alike.

Ch. Indeed! Then among these 25,000 brothers perhaps there were scarcely ten who were really in need of it?

E. That might possibly be.

Ch. Then you give to the rich and opulent, who belong to your lodge, assistance, and leave the poor who do not belong to it, to starve! The words of the Lord, "The poor have ye always with you," do not concern you. You support the rich, the poor may starve and freeze. A fine specimen of charity!

E. If the poor had joined the lodge, they would, in case of sickness, receive the same assistance.

Ch. Then your charity extends just as far as the lodge; where that ends, your charity stops too. Where do you find all this in the Bible, that you, for example, without committing sin, can support the rich and leave the poor to hunger and freeze, or that you are right in making the lodge the measure and limit of your charity? No; the Lord Jesus has preached a far better charity, namely, to aid and serve all the poor and needy; as we have opportunity, to do good to all men, and not to limit and mete out our charity as you do. Still another peculiarity of the odd love of you Odd Fellows, I have noticed. Tell me, do you admit sickly or aged persons into your lodge?

E. Sickly persons, such as, for example, suffer from chronic diseases or defects, are not accepted, according to a long-established custom of our order (see Digest, pp. 239, 200); neither, as a rule, are such as are not able to make their living; and persons above fifty years are generally not admitted, only in special cases, and then only as not entitled to aid (see Digest, pp. 241, 250 ff.).

Ch. Why do you not receive such persons?

E. The existence of the respective lodges would be endangered; for our means are not as yet so extensive as to afford the great amount of pecuniary aid such persons require.

Ch. Fine love that! The really needy, such as sickly and aged persons, are therefore, by law and long-established custom of your order, as a maxim, excluded from your "benevolent society"!

E. We can support them without their belonging to the lodge, and that is really done.

Ch. I believe you can; whether it is done, however, and in how far, these are other questions. But I will not judge concerning that; it does not at present concern me. I am mainly speaking about your principles; and, that they are not based upon charity, but only upon selfishness, is clearly to be seen. As you have informed me, the order, in the year 1869—1870, received $2,724,419.46, and in aiding brothers, families and orphans, $859,906.86 were expended. That leaves a surplus of $1,864,-512.60. What has become of this surplus and of the surplus of former years?

E. The order has many other expenses. I will mention, by way of example, only a few. Every lodge must procure a hall, either erecting one itself, and that costs a great deal of money, or renting one, and that is expensive too. Every lodge has its regalia which are also very costly. Every lodge pays its secretary, every State Grand Lodge its Grand Secretary and other grand officers. The Grand Lodge of the United States has its secretary and other employees to pay. The latter receives annually $3,000, and the secretaries of the State Grand Lodges commonly receive from $500 to $2,000.* The traveling expenses of all the officers, when traveling in the service of the order, are also paid. The conventions also cost a great deal of money. The convention of the Grand Lodge, in September, 1873, which was held in Baltimore, and lasted seven days, cost, alone, $16,995.40. For the current expenses (not charities) $47,572.40 were allowed, or more yet, if required.† The Grand Lodge of the United States has also money on interest, but that is, comparatively, no large amount.

Ch. A very simple calculation shows, therefore, that not even the third part of what you pay in is expended in charities. When you, therefore, have paid in, let me say $300 to the lodge, you or your family receive, on an average, $95 back. The $205 which you paid over and above that, are swallowed up by salaries, luxurious buildings and silly regalia, and such tomfoolery. And, as you support far more wealthy and rich, than really poor people, we may assume that when a member has paid in $300, the poor receive, on an average, $15, or $20 at the utmost, therefrom. See! that is your benevolence, when brought to the light! Indeed I cannot imagine how you, a little while ago, could say that joining the lodge was advantageous. It brings nothing but loss upon loss, and makes one guilty of the great injustice, that one gives to the wealthy and withholds from the poor. No; I really thought you had more sense and a better knowledge of

---

* See Minutes of the Grand Lodge of I. O. O. F. of Pennsylvania, 1871, pp. 210, 411, 429.

† Proceedings of Annual Communication of the Grand Lodge of the United States, 1873 pp. 5943 and 5898.

arithmetic! Whoever wants to get rid of his money and to promote injustice, let him join; but who, on the contrary, will not squander his means or further injustice, let him keep away from it.. Can you mention to me one insurance or mutual aid society which is so enormously expensive as yours, where one does not even receive *the third part* of what he has paid in?

E. I am not much acquainted with other insurance societies; but I think you look upon the whole matter in a wrong light. My family might, for example, be in need of $300; then the lodge would give it to them, even if I had not paid in as much. In this case, the assistance would not be too dearly paid for. And when you represent that to be injustice, that we grant support to the wealthy, you are decidedly wrong. The lodge has obligated itself to do so, and would do wrong if it did not meet its obligations.

Ch. You have always boasted of the benevolence of the Order in general, and now, all at once, you take a particular example. That will not do; we must look at the thing in general. Can you dispute the fact, that the lodge does not even expend one-third of its income for benevolent objects?

E. That I certainly cannot do. It is a fact.

Ch. Very good. Then it is proved beyond contradiction that joining the lodge occasions loss upon loss. And if you have obligations toward the rich and wealthy, meet them, for all I care; but I beg you, do not call that benevolence, yea, even a deed of charity. That is an ungodly falsehood. But let us pass on to other points of your so-called benevolence, which are of higher importance than money or money's worth. You said that the lodge, if requested, cares for the education of orphans, and sends them to academies and schools. What kind of schools are they?

E. We have already several academies and schools to which we send them. These institutions are provided with excellent teachers, capable of imparting valuable instruction to the scholars.

Ch. Do they also give religious instruction?

E. A systematic course of religious instruction is not given, but the whole instruction is in a certain sense religious; however, nothing sectarian is taught.

Ch. Is the Bible also used there?

E. For doctrinal purposes, or for the purpose of instruction or as a reading-book it is not used.

Ch. What is, then, taught?

E. The same as is taught in other schools, such as reading, writing, arithmetic, geography, history, and the like; in short, everything that tends to make the children intelligent citizens and upright men, and to qualify them to earn their living in a respectable manner.

Ch. Then you have heathenish schools, such as, for example, the Greeks and Romans had.

E. What! you call our schools heathenish? No; I tell you, the teachers and managers of the schools are Christians and no Heathens.

Ch. Do the teachers and managers belong to the lodge, and are the schools managed and supported by the lodge?

E. Certainly.

Ch. Well, then, they may be Christians by name. But, as the lodge has long since rejected the Lord Jesus Christ, and as each member approves of that and confesses, with the lodge, that he is saved by his works, they are apostate Christians, and not a hair's breadth better than the Heathen. Indeed, I consider them to be still worse than Heathen, because they have the word of God, but do not believe it, and will not be governed by it; and that we cannot say of the Heathen. Do you know what makes a school a Christian school?

E. No; what does?

Ch. When the word of God rules therein, and everything is conducted according to it: Instruction, praise, blame, punishment and reward. When the school considers it its highest aim to instruct the scholars in the word of God and the way to salvation, to lead the children as lambs of Christ to Jesus, to implant in them faith in and love to him, that he may save them. Is that also the highest aim of your schools?

E. I could not say that it is.

Ch. Then you must surely comprehend that your schools are not Christian, but teach and instruct without Christ; therefore they are on a level with the heathen schools of the Greeks and Romans. Do you think you can answer for it, that you allow the children to grow up without God's word and without pointing them to the only Savior of sinners?

E. I do not know. We give them the necessary education in all things pertaining to this life, and leave it to the scholars, at some later period, to form or to choose their own religion.

Ch. Do you think you act in accordance with the word of God by so doing?

E. What passage speaks against it?

Ch. In Matthew 28 : 19, 20 the Lord Jesus says: "Go ye, therefore, and teach all nations, baptizing them in the name of the Father, and of the Son, and of the Holy Ghost: *Teaching them to observe all things whatsoever I have commanded you.*" Do you have your children baptized?

E. To be sure we do.

Ch. Then it is the more your duty to teach them God's word, or to see that it is done. See, here is the express command of Christ: "*Teaching them to observe all things whatsoever I have commanded you.*" Therefore, every one who undertakes to instruct or to educate children, has the express commandment of God, and therefore the sacred duty, to "*teach them to observe all things which Christ commanded.*" What Christ has commanded is contained in the holy Scriptures, and it is the express command of God that we impress the doctrines of the holy Scriptures on the children's minds. And, that this must be done while they are children, and that we dare not delay it until they are grown up, we learn from many other passages; for example, Mark 10 : 14 : "Suffer the little children to come unto me, and forbid them not." Eph. 6 : 4 : "Ye fathers, bring them up (your children) in the nurture and admonition of the Lord." Joh 19 : 15; Deut. 6 : 7; Ps. 78 : 3, 4. Oh, I shudder when I think of the threefold, grave sin you commit in your schools against God, against the poor children and against yourselves. You sin frightfully against God, in acting in direct opposition to his plain command. You sin in an unjustifiable manner against the poor children, when you, instead of leading them to Jesus, keep them away from him; instead of teaching them the way to Heaven, namely, repentance and faith, conduct them in the damnable way of self-righteousness! Oh, never, never can you answer for it before the judgment seat of Christ. Believe me, these children, who are led astray by you and kept away from Christ, willl rise up against you in the judgment day, and wherewith will you justify yourselves? Having offended the little ones who believed in Christ, the dread sentence must be passed on you which the Lord announces in Matt. 18 : 6. You also sin no less terribly against yourselves, against your own immortal souls, which you, by such disobedience toward God, deliver to eternal condemnation. Oh, I entreat you to reflect, before it is too late.

E. Well, I do not know that it is quite so bad.

Ch. Believe me, it is so bad, yea, even much worse than I am able to tell you. But to another point. You have also reckoned among the benefactions of the order, that the lodge teaches its members to know God, his will, and their duties toward him. And so it is said also in your books. To be sure, I said something about it a while ago, but it can do no harm to recur to it. You surely do not mean to say that the lodge teaches to know the Triune God?

E. I do not mean to say that. It teaches to know one God, the Creator and Preserver of the Universe. Should it teach a Triune God, it would thereby enter into the number of Christian sects; but that it will not do. It stands above parties.

Ch. Whence does the lodge derive its knowledge of this one God, Creator and Preserver of the Universe?

E. From nature, reason and the Bible.

Ch. You have therefore learned from nature, by means of your reason, that there is one God. On the contrary, the ancient Greeks and Romans, our heathen forefathers, and other heathen nations, have learned by means of their reason, and from nature, that there is not one, but many Gods. Who, then, is right? The Heathen have reason just as well as you, and live in nature just as well as you do.

E. But we use the Bible, which the heathen nations did not have.

Ch. But you know what kind of a God the Bible teaches, do you not?

E. The Bible teaches a Triune God, as I told you before. The lodge, however, uses only such passages where it is said that God is one. It cannot teach the doctrine of the Triune God, because Jews and others, who do not believe in the Bible, belong to it.

Ch. You confess, therefore, yourself, and are aware that the lodge does not teach the God who has revealed himself unto us in the holy Scriptures. The God of the lodge is therefore none other than "Allah," whom Mahommed teaches. He also borrowed his doctrine concerning God, or rather his idolatry, from Heathenism, Judaism and Christianity. It is, however, an abominable sin to teach another God than the Scriptures do. It is a gross transgression of the first commandment, which the holy and just God cannot leave unpunished. You thereby revolt against the high majesty of God himself, rob him of his honor, tread it under foot, and make an idol of him. Surely the weighty words in Gal. 1 : 8, 9, do also apply to you.

E. Well, for your consolation, I can tell you that very little time is spent in this instruction concerning God. The principal matters that we are occupied with are of quite a different nature.

Ch. That is indeed poor comfort. In reality, it matters very little whether the lodge in every session teaches to know its idol, which every one shapes for himself by means of his reason, or whether it does so once a month or once every year. The curse of false doctrine rests upon you, until you, through the grace of God, are brought to repentance; and that I wish you with my whole heart. You teach, also, to know the will of God; from whence do you derive your knowledge of his will?

E. Why, from the ten commandments, to be sure. They are read, and every one binds himself to live according to them.

Ch. It is shameful that you make use of the ten commandments, and reject the Triune God who gave them. How you continually transgress the first commandment, we have just seen. You lodge members do not keep the second and third a whit better, to say nothing at all about the second table of the law. You continually make use of the biblical name "God," and yet do not believe in him; you profane, therefore, his holy name, and take it in vain. You use the Bible in the lodge, but do not believe its words; is not that shameful profanation and contempt for the word of God? Instead of deeming the word of God holy, willingly hearing and learning it, you abuse it by making use of it and yet not believing it, and, according to your own words, not submitting to its authority. You make use of it in order to give yourselves the semblance of Christianity, that such as still believe in the holy Scripture may think you are good Christians, and may the easier be induced to join. Do you know what is the chief end of the law?

E. Well, what is it?

Ch. That it work in us knowledge of sin, as Paul says (Rom. 3 : 20), "By the law comes the knowledge of sin." And again (Rom. 7 : 7): "I had not known sin but by the law; for I had not known lust, except the law had said, Thou shalt not covet." The law is to reveal to us especially the sinfulness of our own hearts; is to present to us the wrath and the everlasting punishment of God for sin, that we may learn to know ourselves as "lost and condemned sinners," and long for a Savior. Then will the law become unto us what it should be,—a schoolmaster, to bring us unto Christ (Gal. 3 : 24). Then is man ready to receive the Savior of sinners, who offers himself unto him in his word and sacraments. Do they use the ten commandments in this way in the lodge?

E. That is certainly not the case. We make use of them to encourage the members to a moral walk and conversation.

Ch. Then you quite forget the first and most important design of the law, and intend to make men pious by the ten commandments and without Christ. In this you will never succeed. It seems to me just as if a farmer would reap wheat, but sows thorns. He will never attain his end. You use the ten commandments in order to lead a virtuous life; but for this purpose man needs strength, and this strength the law can never give you. Before man is renewed by repentance and faith, he cannot lead a truly virtuous life. Christ alone can enable him to do so. As you thus make use of the ten commandments in the wrong way, you not only overthrow God's ordinance, but you sow even continually the thorny seeds of self-righteousness in the heart of a lodge member. You teach him that he can fulfill the law by his own strength, and refer him continually to himself. No good fruit can grow from such seed. It is the will of God that we should come unto Christ, should remain steadfast in his word and faith until our end. And in order to do this, a knowledge of sin is the first requisite. Whoever does not know his sins, and that he is worthy of condemnation, never comes unto Christ, and can therefore never be saved. Would you therefore make use of the law, use it in the right way, namely, as a mirror to behold and learn to know your true condition, and God's serious punishment of sin, that the law may also become unto you a schoolmaster to lead you unto Christ. In this way the law becomes a blessing, otherwise it is none.

You have repeatedly said, and it is written in your books innumerable times, that you have nothing sectarian. But your entire doctrine is thoroughly sectarian. Not one single sentence, strictly considered, agrees with the word of God. You have invented everything yourselves, and that in direct opposition to God's word; and therefore your whole doctrine is nothing but sectarianism, yea, sectarianism above all others. A *Christian* sect, according to your doctrines, you are not, because you have not one single article of the Christian, that is, the biblical doctrine. But you are a religious, anti-christian sect, by your teachings. If you now represent that also to be one of the benefactions of the order, that two brothers watch by the bedside of the sick and dying, I must entreat the good God to graciously guard me against this benefit. When I am sick and dying, I want the consolations of the divine word and the blessing of believing prayer. The true Odd Fellow, who believes the doctrine of the lodge, can afford me neither. He cannot in faith comfort and strengthen me from God's word, nor pray for me out of a believing heart for Christ's sake. For this I need truly believing Christians, who, by their faith, can comfort and strengthen me out of God's word; can point me to Christ as my only Savior; can repeat to me his consoling promises in the last struggle, which is often a hard one, and pray in the power of the spirit. I pray God that he grant me such in my dying hours.

Although, in my opinion, this ought to suffice to convince you that the lodge does no truly good works, I will yet refer to another thing which you mentioned. Did you not say that the lodge brothers assisted and helped each other whenever it was possible to do so?

E. Certainly I said so, and it is a fact that we do so.

Ch. Well, I see in this respect you are a good Odd Fellow. Your instruction books enjoin this duty upon you, as, for example, Manual, p. 178 ff. 132; Pocket Companion, p. 13,176 ff.; and you have promised the lodge to do so. If you, for instance, should need a workman, and there were two, suppose one was a member of the lodge, but belonged to no Christian congregation and never attended church; the other was a true Christian and member of a church, but did not belong to the lodge; they both alike needed work and were equally skillful; which of these two would you take?

E. I would most assuredly take him who belongs to the lodge, for by so doing I would keep the promise I gave in the lodge, and know that I had a faithful workman. You surely do not consider that a sin, do you?

Ch. Do you know what is written in Gal. 6 : 10 ?

E. No. What is written there?

Ch. "As we have therefore opportunity, let us do good unto all men, *especially unto them who are of the household of faith.*" The word of God, therefore, tells us we should *especially*, that is, firstly, chiefly, particularly, before all things, do good to them that are of the household of faith. But you, and all the members of the lodge, say: No; firstly, chiefly to my brother of the lodge. See; in such cases, if you wish to be a Christian and a member of the lodge at the same time, you cannot help yourself; you must commit sin, act as you will. If you do good firstly and especially to the members of the lodge, you transgress God's holy commandment. If you, on the other hand, do good firstly and especially to your brethren of the household of faith, you break **the promise** given in the lodge. Is that not dreadful, **to be under** necessity to sin? And we know that the wrath of God from heaven is revealed upon all sin and injustice (Rom. 2), and that it is a fearful thing, as a willful transgressor of the word of the Lord, to fall into the hands of a holy and righteous God. Indeed I do not know how I could rest if I belonged to such a society.

We have now, at your wish, tested the "good works" of the order by the light of God's word. It is true, we have not exhausted the subject; but so much we have already seen, that not a single good work stands the test May God in mercy grant that we learn to know his word and his will aright, and through him be delivered from everything that prevents us from living according to his blessed word! Amen!

SIXTH DIALOGUE.

And whatsoever ye shall ask in my name, that will I do, that the Father may be glorified in the Son. John 14 : 13.

Ernest. Judging from your previous expressions, I must conclude that you have still more objections against the lodge. Is it not so?

Christian. Certainly, I have still more.

E. Pray, which are they?

Ch. I would like again to take up one point at a time. Do they pray in your lodge?

E. Yes, the chaplain opens and closes every meeting with prayer. It is expressly recommended by the Grand Lodge of the United States, as you can yourself read in the Digest, p. 342, where it is said: "*It is highly desirable and eminently proper that all lodges should be opened and closed with prayer.*" See also Manual, p. 248 ff.

Ch. Very well: we will suppose you pray to the true God; upon what do you ground the hope that your prayer is heard?

E. I suppose upon this,—that God is our Father and we are his children. We entreat him, as beloved children entreat their affectionate father, and, as God is our Father, he hears our prayer.

Ch. How can you prove that God is your Father and that you are his children? I well know that your books repeat it a hundred times; for instance, Manual, pp. 109, 140, 375, 385, 366, 222,; Pocket Comp., p. 33; but pray, prove it.

E. God created us his children after his own image; therefore we are his children and he is our Father.

Ch. Most assuredly God created our first parents as his children, after his own likeness. But what has become of this likeness of God, and of God's children? Do you not know that our first parents turned away from God unto the devil, were disobedient to God and obeyed the devil? By such disobedience to God and obedience to the devil, men became the servants of the latter, and "are taken captive by him at his will" (2 Tim. 2 : 26). Through sin they became like unto the devil, and have lost their glorious, innate and divine qualities, and in their stead received qualities like the devil's. For example, before the fall they were holy, after it, unholy; before, righteous, afterward, unrighteous. In the place of love to God, entered slavish fear, aversion, yea, even inward hatred; in the place of uprightness came dissimulation and hypocrisy; in the place of truth entered lies. The Lord Jesus however declares (John 8 : 44) all liars to be children of the devil, and the Apostle says (1 John 3 : 8): "He that committeth sin is of the devil." And that the wrath of God and punishment follow sin, we learn from the Scriptures. Where are, then, the children of God, who have a claim to eternal life?

E. You surely will not declare us all together to be the children of the devil?

Ch. That be far from me, to declare this one or that one to be children of the devil. But I do say, as the word of God says, that we by nature are all in the kingdom of darkness (therefore the devil's), in the power of the devil (Acts 26 : 18), and serve him with all our thoughts and deeds. Does not even the Apostle Paul reckon himself, according to his former walk, among those who served the prince of darkness (Eph. 2 : 1–3)? and yet he at that time led an outwardly moral, yea, strictly pure life. As we, therefore, are all by nature children of the devil and of wrath, we cannot possibly believe that we are God's children and will be saved, because he has created us. If we desire to be saved, we must first *become the children of God;* otherwise it is utterly impossible.

E. How, then, can we become children of God?

Ch. The holy Scripture tells us clearly and plainly. In John 1:12 we read: "*As many as received him* (Jesus Christ) *to them gave he power to become the sons of God, even to them that believe on his name, which were born . . . of God.*" Paul testifies (Gal. 3:26): "For ye are all the children of God by faith in Christ Jesus," because, he says, they have "put on Christ." Only through Jesus Christ and the work of redemption that he wrought, can we attain to the adoption as children of God, as the Scripture says (Eph. 1:5): "Having predestinated us unto the adoption of children by Jesus Christ to himself." These texts declare clearly and distinctly, that solely through Christ can we attain to the adoption as children of God. Whoever suffers himself to be called, enlightened and brought to faith by the Holy Spirit, and embraces and accepts Jesus Christ by faith, to him he gives power to become and to remain a child of God. On the contrary, all those who do not believe in Jesus Christ, are not children of God in the true, full sense of the word. And, as the lodge does not believe in Christ, does not and will not recognize him, it does not consist of God's children. God is not their Father, and they are not his children. Do not misunderstand me; I do not mean to say that there are no children of God in the lodge. It can possibly be that here and there a weak soul, that believes in Christ, has been tempted to join the lodge, who does not know its frightful heresies, and therefore does not see the danger. With such, it is a sin of ignorance. But so soon as they come to this knowledge, they will renounce the communion of the lodge and confess Christ.

E. But still it seems to me as if, upon the whole, you consider us to be children of the devil.

Ch. As I said before, the right of judging persons does not belong to me; therefore I cannot and dare not say this or that one is a child of the devil. Every Christian, however, must say, with the Scriptures: Whosoever does not believe in Jesus Christ, is no child of God, but of the devil. Your lodge and your doctrines have their origin in unbelief. Whoever assents to your false doctrines, approves of them, defends and seeks to spread them, knowing that they do not coincide with the Scriptures, *cannot be a child of God.*

E. You began with speaking about praying. What was your motive in doing so?

Ch. I had a twofold motive: 1, to assure myself that the prayer of your lodge is not heard, indeed is sinful for every true Christian; 2, in order to hear once more the witness of the Scriptures that *the lodge has no God.*

E. You think, therefore, that the prayers we offer in the lodge are not heard and answered?

Ch. Certainly. Do you not know, from your Catechism, how we must pray if we wish to be heard?

E. Our Catechism says: In the name of Jesus Christ.

Ch. Well, will you now affirm that your Chaplain, in opening and closing the lodge, at funerals and dedications of lodges, prays in the name of Jesus?

E. No, I will not assert that. He dare not do it. The prayers are prescribed to him, and to the use of these formulas he is limited But I do assert that I pray with the lodge, and think of Jesus Christ in my prayer.

Ch. I am glad you own that the Chaplain, praying at the request of and in obedience to the lodge, does not offer up his prayer in the name of Jesus. It is also too clearly and plainly written so in your books. A large number of so-called prayers are found in them; for example, Manual, p. 241, ff. 466, 469, 473 ff. 505, 507; Pocket Comp., p. 189 ff. 244, 250 ff.; but not one of them is offered in the name of Jesus Christ; and the Chaplain is expressly directed to use these forms in his prayers. In Pocket Comp., p. 166, it says: "His duty is to open and close the meetings with prayer (using *none other than the prescribed form*)." Your book of laws (Digest) also, on page 341, forbids to offer any other than the prescribed prayers. Indeed, should a Chaplain undertake to pray in the name of Jesus, any member need only protest against it, and he must immediately desist from it. As, then, the lodge does not pray in the name of Jesus, and dare not even do so, these prayers are only such as God cannot hear.

E. What do you call praying in the name of Jesus?

Ch. We pray in the name of Jesus when we firmly *rely and rest upon the merits of Christ;* that is, that we approach God in prayer, relying upon the redemption of Christ, present our petition to him, because he graciously has commanded us so to do (has vouchsafed us the honor to dare to pray), and has mercifully promised that he will hear us. Whoever, now, believes in Christ, confides in his promises, and alone for his sake, and not on account of his own righteousness, entreats to be heard and believingly expects it, he prays in the name of Jesus. And such prayer has the express promise that it shall be heard (John 14:13, 14; 16:24). But without faith it is impossible to please God and to pray in such a manner that one's prayer may be granted (Heb. 6:11). As the lodge, however, does not pray in the name of Jesus, it has no promise that it will be heard; indeed God cannot hear you.

E. Why cannot God hear us?

Ch. Because you do not come to him, relying upon Christ's righteousness, but upon your own; you tread his commandments under foot and subvert his ordinances. Your own righteousness, however, before God is nothing but unrighteousness, which he must punish. How can God possibly hear you, when you appear before him deserving punishment, and yet do not seek and entreat pardon and reconciliation through the blood of Christ, but approach him with your so-called "good works," praising and boasting of yourselves. Truly, God would cease to be holy and just, if he would hear you, and that is impossible.

E. And are our prayers even sinful?

Ch. To be sure. Everything that is done, thought or spoken against God's commandments, is sin. God wills that we should call upon him in the name of his dear Son, and only for the sake of the reconciliation which has taken place through him, shall we ask every good thing, for time and eternity. This, however, you neither do nor wish to do. Therefore every one of your prayers is of itself sin. The prayer of the lodge, however, is a double, nay, threefold sin to every Christian who, knowing that we should pray in Jesus' name, nevertheless prays with the lodge contrary to God's commandments and statues, without even once publicly and earnestly protesting against it. Such a one denies his Lord Jesus Christ, who has purchased him, denies his faith, and is worse than a Heathen. The words apply to him: "That servant which knew his lord's will, and prepared not himself, neither did according to his will, shall be beaten with many stripes" (Luke 12:47); and: "Whosoever shall deny me before men, him will I also deny before my Father which is in Heaven" (Matt. 10:33).

E. But I told you that I think of Jesus during prayer.

Ch. That can indeed not exonerate you. By so doing, you confess that you know how Christians ought to pray, and yet always pray with the lodge contrary to the will of God, and silently approve of its false prayers; therefore you deny your faith in the word of God, and by your silence and participation strengthen the ignorant in the error that their prayers are right, and make yourself continually a partaker of other men's sins. As you nevertheless still cling to the church, which many of your lodge members do not, they certainly must think: "If our prayers were not right, Brother Ernst would surely say something about it; but, as he says nothing, our prayers are certainly right and Christian." Thus by your silence you strengthen other souls in their error, and for this there is no excuse. Do you know who alone can pray in the name of Jesus?

E. Of course, only a Christian, who knows and believes in Jesus.

Ch. You are right. A Heathen or Jew cannot pray in the name of Jesus, because he does not believe in Christ. Do you desire still another testimony from your own book, as further proof that the lodge will suffer no prayer in the name of Jesus, indeed no Christian prayer? Then read what is said on page 166 of the Pocket Companion concerning the Chaplain. There it is said, in plain words: "*It is scarcely necessary to add that the Chaplain should be, if not a Christian, at least a moral man.*" Therefore the lodge is satisfied with any Jew or Gentile, any one who denies Christ or despises God, as a Chaplain, provided he leads a moral life, or, in other words, is not guilty of grave offences. There remains, therefore, not a shadow of doubt that the lodge will have no Christian prayer, but only such to which a Heathen, a Jew, or a denier of Christ, *as such*, can assent to. In short, it wants a prayer that Jew and Gentile can say Amen to, a heathenish prayer. That must surely be a dreadful thing to every true Christian.

E. That is indeed too evident for me to raise any forcible objection against it. But before I say anything further, I would beg you to give me the Scripture proof for your other assertion, that the lodge has no God.

Ch. Most willingly. I have repeatedly proved to you that the lodge does not believe in Jesus Christ, does not recognize him to be the Son of God, does not esteem him to be its Savior and Redeemer. But what does the Scripture say of those who do not recognize and honor Jesus as true God? It says (1 John 2:23):

"*Whosoever denieth the Son, the same hath not the Father.*" There are, perhaps, many in the lodge who think they pray to the true God, the Father of our Lord Jesus Christ; but they err grievously. As the lodge does not believe in Christ as *the Son of God*, and consequently has not the Son, therefore the word of God judges *it hath not the Father*. Moreover, in 2 John 5, it is said: "Whosoever transgresseth, and abideth not in the doctrine of Christ, *hath not God*. He that abideth in the doctrine of Christ, he hath both the Father and the Son." The lodge, not having remained in the doctrine of Christ, but having turned aside from it in every respect, indeed teaching the very contrary from what Christ teaches, is judged by the word of God that "*it hath no God.*" The God to whom you pray in the lodge is an idol, a creature of every one's own imagination, which nowhere exists, which can neither help nor save you; least of all, in your dying hour, can comfort you and grant you a happy end. To pray to such an idol of one's imagination or reason, one need not be a Christian; every Jew, Gentile, Turk and denier of Christ can do that. Indeed, true Christians, faithful children of God, are not fit for that, because they are incapable of so grievously transgressing the first and holiest of all commandments. According to the judgment of the sacred Scripture, the lodge has no God. That is frightful! I would be terribly uneasy in such company. Whosoever is without God, is, according to Ephesians 2 : 12, without a Savior and Redeemer, "an alien from the commonwealth of Israel, and a stranger from the covenants of promise, having no hope" of everlasting life. Blessed is he who considers this in time. Our last hour may come very suddenly.

E. In the light of these plain texts, one can hardly judge otherwise. But before you proceed, I would like to mention something else, which has caused me great uneasiness since our last conversation.

Ch. What is it?

E. From Gal. 6 : 10 I have learned that we, as Christians, should first do good to those that are of the household of faith. Hitherto I have not done so. One case, in particular, oppresses me. Several years ago, I had need of a workman for a length of time. There were two to be had. The one was very poor, had a large family, was a member of the church, attended church regularly, and seemed to be a pious man ; at least, I never heard any evil of him ; but he was not a member of the lodge. The other made a good living, seldom went to a church, and, as I learned afterwards, believed neither in God, Heaven nor Hell. But, because he was a lodge-member, I employed him instead of the other. At that time, I did not feel any great uneasiness about it. I know very well that my conscience reproved me, but I quieted its scruples with the promise I had made on entering the lodge, to support, aid and assist the brethren. I even said to myself : Why did he not join the lodge ? then I could have employed him. The poor man came into great distress, because he was for a long time out of work. His wife, who seemed to be of a somewhat fretful temperament, often shed bitter tears, when she did not know what she and her little ones should eat. Times being hard, and little work to be had, he could only, with great pains and trouble, procure a scanty support for his family. At length, he sold out everything, even to his beds, to procure the necessary means for removing to another State. I am now very sorry for having acted so at that time. I wish I had done otherwise. I have certainly done wrong, have I not ?

Ch. Alas, you have greatly sinned. You have committed a twofold wrong. In the first place, you have acted contrary to the word of God, which says we should especially do good to them which are of the household of faith ; and secondly, you have sinned against charity, by giving employment and bread to him who needed it the least. Charity aids and assists, first of all, those who stand most in need of it.

E. I am truly sorry for it, and it burdens my conscience. I should like to have your advice what I should do.

Ch. In the first place, I would advise you earnestly to entreat God to forgive you, and then —— "

E. I have already done so, but I find no peace.

Ch. Then the fault lies entirely in yourself, either in your faith or in your understanding. The Lord Jesus has suffered on Calvary for all sins, and has shed his precious blood for this sin of yours also, and will gladly forgive you. Nay, more; he offers you the forgiveness of this sin also, and only desires that you do not reject it.

E. Where does God offer me the forgiveness of this sin also?

Ch. In his blessed word and sacrament. In the Epistle to the Ephesians, 1 : 7, we read : "In whom (Christ) we have redemption through his blood, the forgiveness of sins." These words are spoken to you and to me, and in speaking, or rather causing them to be spoken to us, God brings us forgiveness and offers it to us. Whoever, now, believes these words with his whole heart, enjoys what they indicate and declare, namely, the remission of sins. And, that we should in no wise doubt that such gracious words apply to *all sins,* John writes, in his first Epistle, 1 : 7 : "The blood of Jesus Christ, his Son, cleanseth us from *all* sin." Not a single sin, be it great or small, wilfully or ignorantly committed, is excepted. The Lord Jesus has suffered for all sins and for all sinners. Whoever sincerely repents of his sins, and believes in Christ with his whole heart, enjoys, through such faith, the forgiveness of them. In the Communion we receive likewise forgiveness of sins. But why should I explain it to you any further? You know your Catechism, and it teaches us from the Scriptures, that through these words in the Sacrament, the remission of sins, life and salvation, are imparted. If, now, in spite of such a declaration on the part of our God, we cannot enjoy peace, the fault certainly does not lie with him, but with ourselves, in that we in some way or other hinder the grace of God.

E. It comforts me to hear such words of Scripture; but it always seems as if they did not apply to me. I might have known at that time, yes, in a certain sense I did know, that my way of acting was wrong; and yet I laid more weight upon the promise given to the lodge than upon the word of God. I think I am too wicked for God to forgive me.

Ch. It seems to me you are greatly mistaken. You probably imagine that if you had always lived virtuously, and had acted differently in this case also, then God could forgive all those errors that may yet cling to your otherwise good works; do you not?

E. Those are about my thoughts.

Ch. But then you rely, for the forgiveness of your sins, not upon Christ's blood and righteousness, but upon your own merit. So long as you continue in the belief that you need forgiveness merely for this sin, and perhaps a few other faults, but not for your whole life, you will never enjoy peace. We must learn that all our own righteousness, all our best works, before God are but as filthy and polluted rags, something which condemns us before God, because everything, even the greatest virtues, are contaminated and defiled by the sin which continually besets us and cleaves to all we do. We must cast ourselves entirely into the depths of mercy, and say: I come, Lord, not relying upon my own righteousness, but upon thy great compassion; forgive me, *solely for Jesus' sake*, all my sins, even such and such a one. Only pray for a right knowledge of your sins, and for saving faith; make diligent use of the Word of God and the Sacrament, and you will find peace also in regard to the wrong you have done the poor man.

E. I would like to show the man a kindness now, and make amends for my error.

Ch. It is certainly just and proper to make restitution to our neighbor, as far as possible. It is, at all events, in accordance with the word of the Lord, in Ezek. 33 : 14, 15. But I must call your attention to a dangerous error, which easily creeps into the minds of men. We too readily believe that by making what is called amends of the wrong done, we reconcile God, and have made restitution for our sin before God, or, at least, have made God willing to forgive us. That can never be done. We cannot make amends for any sin *before God*, nor can we induce him to forgive us; Christ alone can do that. Love to our neighbor demands that we should indemnify him for the injury done; and therefore no true Christian can or should neglect to do so. However, we dare not imagine that we have thereby canceled the sin and need no further forgiveness. The sin having been committed, we must have forgiveness, and seek that alone in the blood and wounds of Christ. Do you know where the man lives at present?

E. I only know the State to which he moved. Did I know his address, I would immediately write to him. But perhaps I can ascertain that, as I have a brother and several acquaintances residing in the same State. I will write to them to-morrow.

Ch. Do so; and I wish you may find him and have an opportunity of showing him your affection. It is a great mercy of God, when we, by his word, come to a knowledge of our sins, and become sensible of the wrong we have done our neighbor. Being conscious of it, we can pray for grace and pardon, which naturally we cannot do when we are unconscious of it. But the sins we commit against God are much greater and more grievous than those we commit against men. God is the highest majesty; we are indebted to him for all that we have; therefore the sins against him are much greater and more heinous. Therefore if you, by your participation therein, have continually approved of the false doctrine of the lodge; have not confessed Christ; consequently have denied your Lord, his word and the faith, this sin is much greater than those you have committed against men. But generally we are very slow to believe that. May God, in his grace, grant us his holy spirit, that we may, in *every particular*, attain to a right knowledge!

SEVENTH DIALOGUE.

> Then said Jesus to those Jews which believed in him, If ye continue in my word, then are ye my disciples indeed. John 8 : 31.

Christian. You look very much pleased this evening, neighbor. I have been expecting another visit from you this long time. I am very glad that you have come.

Ernest. God be praised, I am indeed very much pleased. The very next day after our last conversation, I wrote to my brother and several acquaintances for the address of that man, whom I shall call N. I received it shortly afterward, and wrote him a long letter, in which I communicated to him that I had done him great wrong at that time by not employing him, who needed it so sadly, but another, who without this work had a good support; that I had acted in this manner because the latter belonged to the lodge and he did not. Certainly no law could punish me for so doing, but I had sinned against charity. I also wrote, that at that time I had not clearly known that it was sin; but had soon quieted my conscience by reminding it that, upon joining the lodge, I had promised to assist and aid all the members; but now, through the grace of God, I had come to a better knowledge. I was now very sorry for my error, and begged his forgiveness. I also enclosed a check for fifty dollars, and entreated him to accept it as a compensation for the injury done. Thereupon, he wrote me this lengthy and beautiful letter. I will read it for you, if you like.

Ch. Pray do so.

E. ESTEEMED MR. ERNEST :—The grace of God be with you! Your affectionate letter caused me to give grateful thanks to God. When I contemplate the faithful love of our Shepherd, Jesus Christ, which so clearly shines forth from your letter, I could not refrain from tears. To God be praise and thanks, that you, through his grace, have been brought to the knowledge that membership in the lodge, to say the very least, *is a very dangerous thing*, and a terrible obstacle to the Christian in the narrow way to Heaven. I was also so unfortunate, at one time, as to allow myself, by all manner of deceptions, particularly by promises of valuable worldly advantages, to be induced to join. After my application for acceptance, I could not sleep for several nights, and when I was admitted, I suffered truly the anguish of hell. They seek, indeed, to make it very terrible and awe-inspiring, by means of darkness, sudden light, frightful pictures, clattering, and the like. My fear, however, was not caused by this hocus pocus, but by my conscience, which bitterly reproached me. Not one evening did I sit in the lodge with a quiet conscience. I knew that quite a number of infidels belonged to it; I knew also that it is written : "*Be ye not unequally yoked together with unbelievers; for what fellowship hath righteousness with unrighteousness? and what communion hath light with darkness? And what concord hath Christ with Belial? or what part hath he that believeth with an infidel? Wherefore, come out from among them, and be ye separate, saith the Lord*" (2 Cor. 6 : 14–17). The conviction that this action was in contradiction to the word of God, tormented me. All the sorry comfort with which a brother tried to console me,—that the lodge let every one believe what he pleased, and had, properly speaking, nothing at all to do with religion, but was merely an association for mutual aid and alleviation of distress,—

could not help me. I found upon almost every page of the publications and books of the lodge, this false comfort refuted, partly in a direct and partly in an indirect manner; therefore my uneasiness remained. But, by the grace of God, I was soon to be brought to a decision. One evening, shortly after the election of a new chaplain, he closed the lodge with prayer in the name of Jesus, entreating God to answer for the sake of Jesus Christ his Son. At the very next meeting, several members made complaint about it. The matter was discussed. I endeavored to prove from Scripture, that it was a Christian's duty to pray in the name of Jesus, and that we could not hope to be heard only on account of the redemption of God's Son. But what answer, dear Mr. Ernst, do you think they gave me? One said we had nothing to do with the Christian religion. The lodge had its own religion, and in accordance with this we pray to God. The lodge had nothing at all to do with Jesus Christ. At home, every one could pray as he pleased; but here in the lodge, no prayer dare or could ever be offered in the name of Jesus; it was also forbidden in the Digest (page 341). Another was more outspoken yet. He declared that he could not conceive how it was possible that there were still people, in our century, who believed the priests' fraud that Jesus was the Son of God. Least of all, could he comprehend that members of the lodge still did so, as the lodge was an educational institution, and purposed to banish all superstition (meaning faith in Christ). Christ, he said further, was a man like one of us; indeed he was of illegitimate birth, therefore a bastard! I was terrified and shocked at such blasphemy. My resolution was taken. When I once more gained the floor, I announced my withdrawal, with the remark that the outspoken infidelity and blasphemy compelled me, as a Christian, to go out from such a society. I anticipated the hatred of most of the members, and it has richly been poured out upon me. They tried to deprive me of my employment and means of living, or to diminish them. At last I preferred to go out of the way of these people, and came into your section of country. Even there, God would not that I should earn my bread in peace. Again I pulled up my stakes, and came hither. Here, through the grace of God, I have not only succeeded in earning an honest livelihood, but something more and above. I already own a fine farm, which is mostly paid for. God be praised, everything goes well with me here. We have also a neat church, a faithful pastor, and the word of God and his sacraments pure and unadulterated, as well as a good school with an excellent teacher for our children. That lodge, in which I, alas! was once a member, resolved that prayer should only be held according to the prescribed form, therefore not in the name of Jesus. I was, however, not the only one who left at that time. The Chaplain, for the same reason, at the next session announced his withdrawal.

I found it quite natural that, at that time, you should employ the other man instead of me, as I, from my own experience, knew the lodge and its aims. I heartily forgave you, and never held a grudge against you on that account. The want of employment at that time, if I look at it right, was of no damage to me. I have experienced the truth of the words of Scripture: "It is good for me that I have been afflicted" (Ps. 119 : 71). I have also experienced that in the old proverb, "Necessity teaches us to pray," a profound truth is concealed. I was driven, by my affliction, to more earnest prayer and into the word of God, and in this way it became a blessing to me.

And now, in regard to the fifty dollars you so kindly sent me, I think it would be a sin to accept pay for this blessing (for indeed the tribulation proved only a blessing to me). If you are agreed, I will double the sum and send it to the Theological Seminary in N—— N———. Pray let me know your opinion as soon as possible.

Thanks be to the faithful God, who has granted us all manner of heavenly blessings, through Christ. May he grant further grace, that we learn to know his word aright and to live in accordance with it. Wishing you the blessing of God, I commend myself to your love and remembrance in your prayers.

Yours, N.

Ch. This letter tunes one's heart to praise and gratitude, and affords us another evidence of the great love of God, who wills not that any one should be lost. Did he not go after this N., and gave him no rest in the communion of the unbelievers, until he came out from among them? Yes; honor and praise be to God, that he follows and seeks us in our wanderings, as a shepherd seeks the straying lamb! Did he leave us to ourselves, we would all be heirs of everlasting perdition.

E. This letter occasions me great joy. He has forgiven me; everything goes well with him. He will not accept the fifty dollars, but will double it and send it to the Theological Seminary in case I consent to it. Well, I think I shall give my entire assent to it. What do you think?

Ch. I think it is the very best thing you can do. This country is in great want of faithful ministers and school teachers. However, such institutions can only be sustained by the loving care of the congregations, and it is our duty, as Dr. Luther so pressingly admonishes us, to do all in our power that the word of God may be handed down pure and unadulterated to those that come after us; therefore it is not only laudable and right, but also our sacred obligation, to support such institutions.

E. N., too, was, then, at one time a lodge member, and went out from it. I was not aware of it before. I, too, have been for some time uneasy about my membership. I do not exactly know what to do. Sometimes I think it is not right to remain any longer in the lodge; at other times the thought arises in me: Should you remain, you might help to change some things for the better. Then again I think: You should withdraw; it is an alliance of unbelievers. Sometimes again it is very hard for me to entertain the thought of leaving, as I have very good friends among them. At other times, the care for my family troubles me, should we meet with misfortune and lose a great deal, or perhaps everything; and if I should die, they would, of course, receive no aid, and the money I have paid in for so many years would be thrown away.

Ch. That you have such scruples and are inwardly tossed from one side to the other, I can well understand. That is one of the struggles between the flesh and the Spirit, between sin and righteousness, between the old and the new man. This struggle is allotted to us. Blessed are we if the Spirit gains the victory (Gal. 5 : 16, 17, 22–24). Should you, however, really believe, that by remaining in the lodge, you would be able to change some things for the better, you would be greatly mistaken. A society with such false doctrine and erroneous belief can never more be cured by remaining in it and meaning to testify against its faults. Even if by our words we would seemingly effect some good, we would by sinfully remaining in it do ten times greater harm. How can the reproof be sincere, or how should others be able to regard it seriously, when they see that he who finds fault quietly remains in the society? No; if there be any means by which such an association can be cured, it is surely only by withdrawing from it, with a clear statement of its false doctrine, and then to seek by word and deed to convince other souls that are captivated by it, of their wrong. However, I believe it is not necessary to waste many words about it. If I might offer my advice, it would be this: Come out from among the communion of unbelievers; or, Renounce the world, cleave to Christ! Yet I should be sorry were you to take this step on account of human persuasion. Coninue faithfully to compare the doctrines of the lodge with the Holy Scriptures, to use the means of grace diligently, entreat the Holy Ghost for enlightenment, and then you will speedily come to a decision. Least of all will the ties of friendship or the money paid in, then keep you back. All these are only earthly and perishable goods. I think we will meanwhile commend this matter to our faithful God and pray that he may direct it so that it may redound to his glory. I believe, however, it would be well for us to talk about some other matters.

I lately read in the Book of Concord of our Lutheran Church, where it speaks in the Epitome of the rule and standard of doctrine and faith: "We believe, teach and confess, that the only rule and standard, according to which all doctrines and teachers alike ought to be tried and judged, are the prophetic and apostolic Scriptures of the Old and New Testaments alone." And it struck me that the lodge has an entirely different rule and standard of doctrine and faith, than the Church of God.

E. The Book of Concord,—what kind of book is that?

Ch. The Book of Concord contains all the confessional writings of our Evangelical Lutheran Church, namely, the three Œcumenical Confessions of Faith, the Augsburg Confession, with its Apology, the Smalcald Articles, the smaller and larger Catechisms of Luther, and the Formula of Concord. Every Lutheran should surely have and diligently read it, that he may know what his church believes, teaches and confesses, according to the Word of God, and what she, according to the Scriptures, rejects as false doctrine. Are you not acquainted with the book?

E. I am acquainted with the Smaller Catechism and the Augsburg Confession, but I do not know the other writings.

Ch. If you wish to read it, I will gladly lend you my Book of Concord, but it is better that you should purchase one for yourself.

E. I shall do so. But you were saying that the lodge has an entirely different standard of doctrine than the Church. I interrupted you. Pray, continue.

Ch. The Church of Jesus Christ confesses the Scriptures of the Old and New Testaments to be the *only* rule and standard of faith, of doctrine and of life, and has expressly declared so in her confessional writings. Does the lodge do the same? No; it has an entirely different rule and standard of faith, doctrine and life, namely, conscience; indeed not the conscience enlightened by and resting in the word of God, but *the conscience corrupted, perverted, darkened and led astray by sin*. For so we read in the Manual, p. 376: "*The authority of conscience, in* RELIGION, must be PARAMOUNT." In the Pocket Companion, p. 127, it says: "Conscience should be permitted always *to govern us*, and as it directs, *so should we ever act*." Here it is clearly and unmistakably said, that the lodge does not recognize the Word of God as superior to conscience. It does not give the Word of God the first place, but conscience; does not allow conscience to be corrected, enlightened and quickened by God's Word, but places the Word of God far, far beneath conscience, and subjects it to its reason and egotism. Thus, whatever the Heathen's conscience tells him, in religious matters, that is right; what his conscience whispers to him that rejects Christ, is also right; but what the conscience of the believing Christian. after it has been enlightened and quickened by the Word of God, tells him concerning religion, that is called "sectarianism." And why is all that right which the conscience of those says who do not believe in the Bible? Because the highest authority which the lodge has, has declared it to be so. What a piece of blasphemous folly! Truth, in religious matters, is but *one*. Two contradictory doctrines cannot both be true. What a confusion of doctrines this would make! Let us take, for example, the doctrine concerning God. The Jew declares: I believe, according to my conscience, in one only invisible God, but not in a triune Being. Here the highest authority has spoken. Our Indian says: I believe, according to my conscience, in the Great Spirit and in evil spirits. Here the highest authority has spoken. The Chinese declare, pointing to a small idol: This is my household God, in whom I believe, according to my conscience. Here again the highest authority has spoken. The Fetish worshiper has a potsherd hanging on the wall, and solemnly affirms: According to my conscience, this is my God, whom I adore. Here the highest authority again has spoken. The Mohammedan, with pious mien, says: Allah, according to my conscience, is my God, and Mohammed is his prophet. Again the highest authority has spoken. Finally, the unbeliever declares: Nature is God, and there is none other; that is my belief, according to my conscience; he is a fool who believes otherwise. Here, too, the highest authority has spoken. Now tell me which of all these contradictory doctrines is right? The highest authority has spoken in regard to all. As they contradict each other and no two of them agree, whom shall and can one believe? Behold! the only truth existing becomes a twenty-fold truth, continually contradicting itself. Is not that dreadful?

E. My understanding of this matter, until now, has been, that the conscience of each individual should decide in regard to his religion.

Ch. This is probably meant, and I understand it so; and in this way we get a truth of a thousand shades, and contradicting itself in a thousandfold manner. There is, however, but one faith, one doctrine, one God (Eph. 4:3–6). But the reason of it is, that the lodge does not recognize the Word of God to be above conscience, but, on the contrary, elevates conscience far above God's word, and allows this conscience, thus sundered from God's word, to judge and decide on all faith and doctrine. Should the lodge, for example, say: The Word of God is the only rule and standard of faith, doctrine and life; let your conscience be ruled and quickened thereby, and then never act against the dictates of your *conscience, resting in God's word,*—it would do right. But that it will not do; neither can it do so, with its mongrel religion, to which the Jews, Heathen and unbelievers agree. The majesty of God and of his holy word is terribly dishonored and desecrated in this way. Sinful and ungodly men set their perverted conscience in place of God's everlasting word. What do you now think of this absurd principle of the lodge, that conscience, unenlightened by the Word of God, should, in religious matters, decide all things? Do you consider that to be right?

E. I do not believe that it is correct, and must say, that in its application, it shakes and overthrows every real truth. I, at least, can no longer consent to it.

Ch. Were this principle correct, then it was unnecessary for God to give the ten commandments and send the prophets and his Word; for, if conscience, without God's word, is the highest authority, what is the use of them all? The sufferings and death of Jesus Christ, whereby he redeemed the world and taught the way to heaven, would then be just as useless and superfluous, because, according to that principle, the natural conscience, without God's word, teaches men the right way, that is, the way to Heaven. If we now look into the holy Scriptures, we find, that by nature we know nothing of God and divine things, as we ought to know in order to be saved. In 1 Cor. 2 : 14, it is said, for example : "But the natural man (that is, man as he is born into the world, as he is by nature) receiveth not the things of the spirit of God; for they are foolishness unto him : neither can he know them, because they are spiritually discerned." Here, not only all true knowledge, all right understanding of spiritual things, are denied to the natural man, but also the power to seize and comprehend them, even when they are communicated to him. In Matt. 11 : 27, the Lord Jesus says : "No man knoweth the Son, but the Father; neither knoweth any man the Father, save the Son, and he to whomsoever the Son will reveal him." Here we see, therefore, that we can in no wise know God the Father, unless the Son does reveal him to us in the Word. And when Peter confesses, "Thou art the Christ, the Son of the living God," Christ answers: "Flesh and blood hath not revealed it unto thee, but my Father which is in Heaven" (Matt. 16 : 16, 17). Thus we see, that of ourselves, we are unable to know either the Father or the Son, or other spiritual things, without the divine revelation. God must give us the knowledge of salvation (Luke 1 : 77), by giving us "the spirit of wisdom and revelation in the knowledge of him" (Eph. 1 : 17). As little as we, of ourselves, can know God by our conscience, so little can we, by our conscience, learn the way to Heaven. The conscience of no natural man has ever taught him: Repent and believe in the Gospel. There have been, for example, learned men among the Heathen, particularly among the Greeks and Romans, and every one of them possessed a conscience; but not a single one has ever taught: Believe in the Lord Jesus Christ, and you shall be saved. Indeed, this doctrine which the lodge has established, is ruinous, and no one who follows it can be saved.

E. I firmly believe that, in religious matters, we can only allow the sacred Scriptures to be the rule and standard; otherwise we fall into pernicious confusion, from which we cannot extricate ourselves. Every one claims, according to his conscience, to have the right religion.

Ch. We fall not only into wretched confusion, but, what is surely still worse, we cannot be saved, as conscience, without the word of God, never finds the right way of repentance and faith. When, however, the lodge assigns to conscience the highest authority in affairs of religion, it means to apply this only to the lodge members, and all such as accept its false doctrine; a conscience that in matters of religion differs from its conscience, it does not respect. I, for example, according to my conscience, which rests in God's word, can only warn against the pernicious doctrines of the lodge. Thus my conscience teaches me, because it is so instructed by the Word of God. The Pocket Companion, on page 127, says: "Conscience should be permitted always to govern us; and as it directs, so should we ever act." Accordingly, we should think the lodge would respect that, and say: This man is, no doubt, honest, and acts according to his conscience, according to his highest authority. But how do you think the lodge treats those who contradict its false doctrines? It abuses them in the most vulgar terms, although it pretends to be very respectable. The lodge calls me, because, for conscience sake, I am compelled to warn against its false doctrines, on page 182 of the Pocket Companion, "base" and "unworthy." It pretends, therefore, to allow liberty of conscience, but exercises terrible tyranny over the conscience. Every one who opposes its false doctrine, and must do so for conscience sake, is abused as "base" and "unworthy." What would it perhaps do, if it should obtain the exclusive control of the religion of States? Undoubtedly the time of bloody persecution would return. Verily, we have reason to pray also in regard to this enemy of our faith: "Rise up, Lord, and let thine enemies be scattered" (Numb. 10:35). And: "Return, we beseech thee, O God of Hosts: look down from heaven, and behold, and visit this vine; and the vineyard which thy right hand hath planted, and the branch that thou madest strong for thyself" (Ps. 80:14, 15). Yes, that is the main object of the lodge, particularly of the initiated and leading personalities, to thrust Jesus Christ, slyly and most imperceptibly, from his throne, that is, to remove him from the hearts and homes, from the churches and schools.

EIGHTH DIALOGUE.

That Christ may dwell in your hearts by faith, that ye be rooted and grounded in love. Eph. 3 : 17.

Ernest. Since our last conversation, I have reflected much upon your last words. You said, namely, that the lodge labored to dislodge Christ from his throne, to remove him from the hearts and homes, churches and schools. When I now reflect on my experience in the lodge; on everything that was spoken, considered, resolved and done, I must confess that much has occurred which, as a Christian, one cannot approve of. But where is there a society, of any size, in which much that is unchristian does not occur? Is it not the case even with Christian congregations? But I must say that I have never witnessed that on the part of the lodge it was ever resolved or declared: We will extinguish Christ or Christianity.

Christian. I believe, very readily, that you have never heard such declarations or resolutions of the lodge. One does not do it so bluntly. It would be very fortunate for Christians, especially for such as are weak in Christian knowledge, if the lodge would speak out honestly and openly and declare: We will have nothing to do with Christ; we will go to heaven by our own merits; we therefore reject the doctrine of redemption through the blood and death of Christ, the doctrine of repentance and faith; indeed it is our mission to abolish Christianity from the earth. I repeat, it would be very fortunate were the lodge openly to come out with these its secret projects. Then the eyes of the simple would be opened, and no Christian possessed of a spark of Christianity would join the lodge. It would then be over with the spread of the lodge among Christians; and, as up to the present it has manifested no inclination to propagate its peculiar tenets among the wild Bushmen of Africa and the Cannibals of New Zealand, their very existence would be at stake. The leaders are well aware of this fact, and therefore never express themselves openly and honestly. The Devil, this seducer from the beginning, has ever acted in the same way. Do you believe that Adam and Eve would have ever suffered themselves to be tempted to sin by the Devil, had he come out openly with his secret designs? If, for example, the Devil had said: Here, Eve, eat of the fruit of this tree; it tastes good, but your eating will bring upon you the wrath of God, all kinds of temporal misery, will rob you of the peace of God; will deliver you, after much sickness and suffering, unto death, and after death will plunge you into the everlasting torments of hell,—what do you think, would Eve have eaten of the fruit?

E. Most assuredly not.

Ch. About as much success would the lodge have among Christians, if it came out openly with its designs, as it should, according to its own motto. This it knows very well, and therefore seeks, in a very subtle manner, to extirpate Christianity; and behold, it is only too frequently successful in its efforts. The Devil, by means of cunning lies and frauds, also succeeded in seducing our first parents, and succeeds daily in leading astray their descendants.

E. How, then, do you think the lodge goes to work?

Ch. Not by such resolutions. You can rummage all the writings of the lodge, and will scarcely find such a resolution. I have already read a great mass of publications of the lodge and of its members, not alone those which you brought me, but many other books and writings, which I found advertised therein, and have sent for, but have never found such a resolution. It would indeed be the beginning of the end of the lodge. It works in a very different way. It assumes a Christian appearance, and tries to maintain it. It deceives the Christians whom it wishes to win for the lodge, by pretending that the lodge lays great stress upon Christianity, that it has even done a great deal to uphold the knowledge of God and the Christian religion, as it so frequently boasted of in your publications; for example, Manual, p. 130 ff., where it is said such associations were "*mighty agents in preserving and perpetuating a knowledge of the truth, as regards both* GOD *and man.*" As further proof that the lodge promotes Christianity, they are told that the open Bible lies always upon the table (see Proceedings Grand Lodge of Wisconsin, 1871, p. 1533), that the Ten Commandments are read to every one who is initiated; that on conferring of the degrees, at funerals, laying of cornerstones, dedication of lodges, &c., &c., portions of the Bible are read and applied; that the lodge is opened and closed with prayer; further, that it is precisely the lodge which performs good Christian works, which the congregations ought to do, but neglected, namely, to assist the widows and orphans, to visit and relieve the sick, and to bury the dead. And probably it is reiterated a hundred times, as, for example, in Heart and Hand of July 22, 1871, p. 119, that in their secrets and their whole nature there is nothing contradictory to our duties toward God, our neighbor and ourselves. And just under this pious pretext, the lodge labors, with all its might, to extirpate Christianity. And that ——

E. But how does it set about it, then?

Ch. Well, in the first place, tell me in what consists *true* Christianity.

E. I could not, perhaps, better express it in a few words, than by saying: In faith in Christ Jesus, in love to him and childlike obedience.

Ch. Therefore the sum and substance of Christianity is Jesus Christ, is he not?

E. Certainly. The very name "Christian" designates one who believes in, loves and follows Jesus.

Ch. Very well. Now, nothing less than this center of all Christianity, the lodge attempts to do away with, *in making Jesus Christ entirely superfluous to the members of the lodge.* On every page of the writings of the lodge, we read that man, in himself, has the ability to make himself a moral man and a citizen and heir of heaven. The lodge declares "*the most important uses and aims of Oddfellowship to be, the imbuing of the minds of our brethren with proper conceptions of their powers and capacities*" (Man. p. 112 ff.); "*to imbue him with conceptions of his capability for good*" (Man. p. 47 ff.); that a "true Odd Fellow" belongs "to the highest style of man" (p. 269), and that such live "*with a conscience void of offence toward God and man,*" and "*their departure from earth is but a translation to a blissful immortality*" (p. 157), in order to rest "in that angel land" (Pocket Comp. p. 182). Now tell me, has he who believes this, still any need of Jesus?

E. I cannot see why such should have any need of Jesus as heir Savior.

Ch. It is certain, first and above all things, we need the Lord Jesus for the forgiveness of sins, as his blood alone cleanses us from sin (1 John 1:7). But all those who believe what the lodge teaches, have no need of Christ for the forgiveness of sins; for they do not know that they are poor sinners, worthy of condemnation, but do all they can to prevent the knowledge of sin, to stifle the convictions of sin, and even profess that they live "with a conscience void of offence toward God and man," while the Scriptures say (Rom. 3:23): "For all have sinned," and are all, "by nature, the children of wrath" (Eph. 2:3), and: "There is none that doeth good, no, not one" (Rom. 3:12). Is it not horrible to read such derision of the sacred word of God? If we, for example, consider the first commandment, in which, among other things, it is said that we should love God *above all things*, and examine ourselves whether we really do so, we certainly are constrained, with Dr. Luther, to say, that we transgress this commandment every hour and minute, because we never *love God as we ought to love him*. Our conscience is therefore not free from offence toward God, according to this one commandment. In spite of this, the lodge asserts the contrary, and declares: Our conscience is void of offence toward God. Unto every one, then, who believes this assertion, the Lord Jesus is the most superfluous object in the world. Behold, this is the way the lodge works to remove the Lord Jesus from the hearts of its members. Let us suppose the case, that such an Odd Fellow is the father of a family; will he be likely to lead his children to Jesus, the Savior of sinners? Will he teach his dear little ones to sing:

> " Jesus' blood and righteousness,
> That is my ornament and dress
> With this before God's throne I'll stand
> When I go to the better land " ?

Will he endeavor to awaken faith in Christ, and instill love to him in the hearts of his children? Certainly not. And if the mother still has faith in Christ, and directs her children to him, he will, to say the least, with a shrug of the shoulder, smile at her stupidity, and in some way manage that the tares of his unbelief do not allow the good seed to spring up in the children's hearts. See! this is the way the Lord Jesus is driven away from the homes. The next consequence is, that he is also removed from the schools and churches, wherever the influence of the lodge extends so far. That you do not teach the Lord Jesus in your orphan schools, you have already confessed. Therefore you have fortunately (?) banished the Lord Jesus from your schools. And when the true Odd Fellows gain the upper hand in a congregation, they soon banish him also from the church; that is, they will not suffer that repentance and conversion, faith and reconciliation through the blood of Jesus, be preached. You can find many such congregations in this country. This false doctrine of self-righteousness is the explanation of the fact that we so very seldom find a Free Mason (whose doctrines are the same as yours) or an Odd Fellow who *really* loves the preaching of the pure gospel,—baptism, absolution and the Lord's supper. It is true, we find, here and there, members of secret societies who contribute largely towards building churches, or defraying the expenses of the congregation; but, that this is not done from love to Christ, they prove by their generally despising the means of grace. Nor can it be otherwise. If I am a "true Odd Fellow," and believe that I can help myself, and by my own virtues merit Heaven, I do not need the assistance of Christ and the means of grace. I cannot possibly still find pleasure in the preaching of repentance and faith. It must be disgusting to me, to hear from the pulpit that I am a poor sinner; intolerable, that I should be called upon to repent; my heart must revolt when I hear that through pure grace I must be saved, and that all my good works *can help me nothing* in getting to Heaven. I am not at all surprised that the majority of the lodge members maintain, or sooner or later will maintain such a position. From *the seed* which is sown in the lodge and all its publications, no other fruit can grow.

E. Do you believe that all think so?

Ch. I hope not; be it far from me to assert that. On the contrary, I believe that there are many in the lodge who do not know or are aware what a terrible association they have joined, who know themselves to be miserable sinners, who believe in Christ and hope to be saved through him. I am only speaking of what the fruit of such sowing is and must be when it springs up, and what general experience teaches. I also believe, most assuredly, that you, since joining the lodge, have often enough experienced, that this sowing of false doctrine has brought forth the sad fruit of disinclination to and inward estrangement from the word of God, in most members.

E. Certainly that is a fact, as I well know, confirmed by experience. I only wanted to hear if you made no exceptions. But, as you do, I can make no objections to what you say.

Ch. Yea, God be praised that there are still exceptions. It is his great mercy that many (as I hope) have a better faith than the lodge teaches. That is certainly no merit of the lodge, but the great compassion of God. Such, however, stand in great danger of soon losing their faith entirely; for such a communion with unbelievers has always a very injurious influence. They make themselves, continually, "partakers of other men's sins," and transgress God's express commandment (2 Cor. 14 : 17). May God, in his mercy, have compassion on these deceived and blinded souls, who are thus led astray, and open their eyes before it is too late.

While I think of it, let me call your attention to the publications of the order and their anti-christian tone. Should I indeed mention all the anti-christian sentiments contained therein, I should really not know where to end. But only a few. The Grand Representative, F. S. Ostheim, who represented the Grand Lodge of Oregon in the Convention of the Grand Lodge of the United States, held in Baltimore in September, 1870, and who soon after went to Germany, wrote, on the 20th of April, a long letter, which is printed in your paper, "The Odd Fellow," in the June number of 1871, p. 369. In this letter, Mr. F. S. Ostheim states that the order had been introduced into Germany, and writes, among other things: "Whether Jew, Turk or Christian, is immaterial to the irrefutable laws of nature, which are based upon reason, just as in general such like *human institutions*, however beneficial their influence may prove, are frequently only calculated to enchain the world in the *shackles of error and prejudice*. A universal brotherhood, on the contrary, presupposes that harmony, which we perceive everywhere in the works of a *latent power which we call God*. The same (the brotherhood of the Odd Fellows, namely, the Author) is therefore divine, is a divine institution, which bids defiance to the intrigues of earthly decrees. The accord of this harmony finds its best expression in our hearts. If the heart beats only for what is good and noble, it needs *no other religion than that which it dictates to itself*. It is *our order* which chiefly promotes these cosmopolitan principles, and therefore its propagation in all civilized countries may of right be considered as of so much greater importance." From these words we see: 1st, that with Mr. Ostheim the religion of a Jew or Turk passes for at least as much, if not more, than that of a Christian; 2d, that he calls the Christian church, with her confession, "a human institution"; therefore does not recognize Jesus Christ, the true God, to have founded the Christian church; indeed, he holds the church, with her doctrines and faith, without expressing it in as many words, to be an institution for spreading ignorance, calculated "to bind the world in the shackles of error and prejudice"; 3d, that he acknowledges no *personal God* who possesses a self-existent being and free motion, but only a "latent (that is, concealed, secret) power," which he calls God. Perhaps Mr. Ostheim imagines this secret power, which he calls God, to be similar to the power of the magnet, which is also secret; we do not see or hear it, but only recognize its existence by the effect, when, namely, a piece of iron is brought near it. As, therefore, the power of the magnet is in man's control, that is, he can allow it to work or not, so, it would seem, Mr. O. represents to himself the imaginary God; that it therefore lies in his power to allow his God to work, and to interfere when he pleases and to prevent it when he pleases. A fine God that! 4th, we see that Mr. O. teaches, no man needs any other religion than what his own heart dictates to him, when it only "beats for what is good and noble." Does Mr. O. recognize the sacred Scriptures as the rule and standard of his religion? By no means! His own heart, which, like every one's heart, is corrupt, perverted, and obscured by sin, is to him the sole rule and standard of his religion; what that "dictates" to him is perfectly sufficient, and certainly, according to his opinion, is also the best. Mr. O. has therefore the same religion which every Heathen, Jew, Turk, unbeliever and scorner of God has. Finally, 5th, we learn therefrom what the lodge really aims at. Mr. O. writes: "It is *our order* which chiefly promotes these cosmopolitan principles (the maxims of universal religion), and therefore its propagation in all civilized countries may of right be considered as of so much greater importance." Therefore the order, particularly its leaders, like this "Grand Representative," are *clearly conscious* that by their "principles" the religion of their own heart, which suits Heathen, Jews, Turks and all unbelievers, will mostly be extended, and true Christianity thereby be exterminated. For this reason, they labor with all zeal to lead souls astray not only in this country, but also in other countries, and for this purpose the order has been transplanted to Germany. In the Manual, pp. 110, 441, and in "The Odd Fellow" for May, 1871, p. 310, it is said that the pecuniary benefits are "scarcely a tithe" of the "aims and objects" of the lodge, indeed that they are only "means to the end." What are, then, the other nine-tenths of their "aims and objects"? The above mentioned number of "The Odd Fellow," page 10, answers this question thus: "It is *the great aim* of the brotherhood of the Odd Fellows ... to give their adherents a correct understanding of the relation between God and man." That means, in plain language, something like this: We will extend our religion, which "our own heart dictates," among our members and as much farther as we possibly can, and we will extirpate the Christian religion, with its Christ, in so far as we are able to do so. We will not have the God of the Bible; we have made one according to our imagination, and we will not allow the Bible to define our relation to him; no, we will do that ourselves, according to the pleasure of our own hearts.

E. Well, God be praised that Mr. Ostheim's religion is not mine.

Ch. What do the papers of the order say, now, to this doctrine of Mr. O., which he plainly enough represents to be the doctrine of the order? Is there in all your papers, numbering about twelve, only *one* dissenting voice to be heard, which says: "No, that is not our doctrine"? Not a single one is to be heard. Nay, still more. This Mr. Ostheim, who has so decidedly spoken as an infidel; who declares that he does not believe in a *personal* God, and recognizes no biblical doctrine, but only that of his own heart;—this infidel is highly extolled in your papers. The editor of your paper, "Heart and Hand," introduces him, for example, in the number of July 15th, 1871, page 109, as his personal friend and brother, and calls the heart, which had made this confession of unbelief, a "noble" one. And, as it was Mr. O. who first proposed the introduction of the order into Germany, and pressed it with all ardor, there is no end to his praise. Truly, whoever knows nothing of the lodge except this confession of Mr. O., knows what it is and what are its designs.

Among the people, it is commonly believed that the Free Masons and Odd Fellows have a covenant with the devil. If by this is meant that they have, in a certain form, given themselves over and bound themselves by a written document to the devil, it is erroneous; but if thereby is meant, that by the false doctrine which they adopt, the devil gradually acquires more and more power over them, blinds them more and more, and leads them away from the path to Heaven, so that at length he gets them entirely in his power, unless God takes compassion upon them, it is entirely correct. This belief of the people contains a profound truth. In reality, it matters very little, whether I give myself up at once to the devil, or whether, by apostacy from Christ, I gradually give him more and more room, so that in the end I become his own. In either case, I am in his power and am his captive (2 Tim. 2 : 26). This sowing of false doctrine must produce evil fruit. Not only that thereby all true faith, all love to God and his word are torn from the heart, but heathenism, similar to that in New Zealand, even if in a more polished form, must gradually grow. The pernicious consequences of such doctrines in social life must more and more come to light, and gradually undermine all truth and faith, all real morality. I will adduce but one example to show in how far that already manifests itself. In the "Odd Fellow" of October, 1870, page 626, the decisions granted by the Grand Sire, in the course of the year, are given. The Grand Sire is, namely, the highest authority of the order, and has to decide on all questions, in the course of the year, and the annual assembly of the Grand Lodge must approve of or reject these decisions. Among others, in the course of the year 1869–1870, the following question was submitted to him: "When a brother renounces Odd Fellowship, whether the lodge can regard it as a resignation from the order; if not, to what extent does it affect his membership? Answer in the *negative, and that such so-called renunciation* of the order has no effect whatever upon his membership or standing in the lodge.*" The Grand Sire, therefore, permits the members of the lodge, when it seems advantageous to them, readily to swear they are not Odd Fellows, and by this decision protects them, so that the lodge to which they belong cannot and *dare* not punish them, by declaring that "such so-called renunciation of the order has no effect whatever upon their membership or standing in the lodge." He thereby not

---

* The "Odd Fellow," a German paper for Odd Fellows, published by M. C. Lilley & Co., Columbus Ohio, uses the word "Abschwoerung"—abjuration.

only approves of *perjury*, but also takes *the perjurer under his protection*. And what has the Grand Lodge of the United States done in regard to this decision? Did it reject it as ungodly, as approving, protecting and promoting the sin of perjury? By no means! It *approved* of this decision, as you can read in Proceedings of the Grand Lodge of the United States, 1870, page 4716, and on page 697 of the "Odd Fellow" of November, 1870. The entire lodge of the Odd Fellows, from the smallest to the greatest, approve hereby of perjury. Every Odd Fellow may now, once or ten times, swear that he is no Odd Fellow and does not belong to the lodge, and what lodge can exclude him on account of this perjury? Not a single one! Indeed no lodge dare undertake to punish him or to make remonstrances against this terrible sin, because, as is expressly said, this "has no effect whatever upon his membership or standing in the lodge." The lodge considers perjury as a trifle, for which no member dare be brought to account. Can one, after all this, believe an Odd Fellow, even under oath? It is impossible for me to do so; for whosoever knowingly and willingly perjures himself in one thing, why should he not always swear falsely, when his heart, which naturally "beats only for what is good and noble, dictates," or when it seems to him to his purpose? A fine specimen of the much lauded "morals" of the Odd Fellows!

E. Is that really said there?

Ch. Here, read it for yourself, and, that you may not think the paper gives a false account, see here, in your Digest the same is said twice, on pages 263 and 368.*

---

* This decision of the "Grand Sire" and its approval can be read in all the reports of the State Grand Lodges and Grand Encampments, at their first sessions after the above mentioned Convention of the Grand Lodge of the United States, which therefore were held in the fall of 1870 or in the following year; for example, Annual Communication of the R. W. Grand

E. I could not have believed that to be possible! There it really stands, and is really so. I read the report of the Grand Lodge of the United States at that time, but this did not at all occur to me; neither did I attach any particular importance to it. But I must say, that I most positively disapprove of and reject such a decision, and can now and never more give my consent to it.

Ch. Well, the Grand Lodge of the United States will give itself very little concern about that. When 400,000 Odd Fellows approve of this decision and one, or, for all I care, a whole half dozen do not agree to it, that would hinder or retard it just as little as a small grain of sand could stop a wagon. It has resolved so, and will uphold its resolution so long as it seems to be politic It has, however, hereby again put on record that it *does not acknowledge* the Word of God, which pronounces heavy punishment on perjury, and that Mr. Ostheim is correct when he says that the lodge only accepts the religion which its own heart dictates. This standard of its religion, namely, its own heart, has "*dictated*" this; its "highest authority," its conscience, approves it, "instructs it so"; therefore it is right. Indeed, one would think that whoever had a spark of Christianity left in him, must be convinced by such facts, that the lodge not only has nothing of God's word, but is thoroughly anti-christian. The devil, however, holds his captives fast and blinds them more and more, that with seeing eyes they do not see. and with hearing ears they do not hear. This decision was laid before all the State Grand Lodges, all the publishers of your papers are acquainted with it.

Lodge I. O. O. F. of Iowa, October, 1870, p. 242 ; Ann. Communication of the Grand Encampment of the same month and year, p. 85 ; Proceedings of the R. W. Grand Lodge of Wisconsin, 1871, p. 1526 ; of the Grand Encampment, 1871, p. 205 ; Minutes of the R. W. Grand Encampment of Pennsylvania, from June, 1870, to May, 1871, p. 16.

Have you ever heard that even *one* State Grand Lodge or *one* paper had opposed it?

E. No, I have not.

Ch. Just as little have I. And this more than sufficiently proves, that they all acknowledge this decision, all approve of and protect *perjury.* "Lo, they have rejected the word of the Lord, and what wisdom *is* in them?" (Jer. 8 : 9). That, however, in spite of such facts, almost every eye of the 400,000 Odd Fellows remains closed, proves again that man, by nature, is entirely darkened, and cannot come to the true knowledge without the enlightening of God the Holy Spirit. But how shall the poor member of the lodge come to knowledge, seeing that the lodge seeks to remove them as far as possible from the Word of God and God's word from them? May God have compassion!

NINTH DIALOGUE.

> I am crucified with Christ; nevertheless I live: yet not I, but Christ liveth in me: and the life which I now live in the flesh I live by the faith of the Son of God, who loved me, and gave himself for me. Gal. 2 : 20.

Christian. Neighbor, you have not shown yourself for a long while. What does that mean? Surely you are not angry with me?

Ernest. No, God be praised, I am not angry with you, but, on the contrary, owe you many thanks. I have had a hard time to go through.

Ch. In what respect?

E. After we had conversed together, for several evenings, about the lodge, it gradually became clear to my mind, that what the lodge teaches is not in unison with the sacred Scriptures. It lasted, however, a good while before I could bring myself to confess it to you. The words of God in Galatians 6 : 10, particularly, threw light on the subject, as well as the approval of the terrible perjury of which we spoke last time. I however always sought to strengthen myself in the opinion that it was not necessary for me to separate from the lodge, because, I said to myself, that by my remaining in it I could perhaps change some things for the better. I also made some slight attempts to do so, but, upon the whole, have had the same experience that N. writes that he did, although in a somewhat milder form. I gradually gained a clearer knowledge of the subject, and learned to understand that the sins of false doctrine, the denial of Christ and of salvation through grace alone, are much worse than those committed against men. I have been especially benefited by the sermons which our minister preached a short time ago, on Romans 3 and 4, wherein he so clearly and plainly proved from the Scriptures, that we can only be saved by grace through the merit of Jesus Christ, that I think everybody must say yea and amen to it. Then my conscience began to reproach me on account of my connection with the lodge, as an alliance of unbelief, and because it teaches contrary to the word of God and professed infidels belong to it, with whom Christians, according to God's word, should have no "communion." The passage (2 Cor. 6:14-17) was day and night in my mind, where it is said: "Be ye separate"; "be ye not unequally yoked together with unbelievers"; and Eph. 5:11: "Have no fellowship with the unfruitful works of darkness, but rather reprove them." The verse, also, which I had learned in my school days, occurred to me: "And that servant which knew his Lord's will and prepared not himself, neither did according to his will, shall be beaten with many stripes." A terrible struggle arose in my heart. Sometimes it was: No; you are a Christian; you can no longer be a member of the lodge, no longer remain in the communion of unbelievers, no longer transgress God's commandment; you should declare your withdrawal. Then again it was: Will you bid adieu to all truly good friends which you have in the lodge, and against whom you have nothing to allege? Will you never visit any more that place where you nevertheless have learned much that was useful? Will you throw away all the money which you have paid in for these many years? No, that will never do! Besides, after all, the thing is not so very bad. Consider how much good the lodge has effected. Many widows and orphans have been assisted, many tears dried, much temporal want prevented. But scarcely had I endeavored in this way to quiet myself, when my conscience cried: "Whoever knew his Lord's will and did it not, shall be beaten with many stripes"! Can you remain there, where your Lord Jesus, who has loved you unto death, and shed his blood for you, is wickedly denied and crucified? Confess your Lord, then he will confess you, not only with words but also in deeds. If you do it not, you deny your Lord, are worse than Peter, make yourself partaker of other men's sins, strengthen by your example your best friends in the delusion that they are in the right way. Separate yourself! have no communion with unbelievers! So the tempest raged in my heart. Then I determined once more to examine the matter quietly and thoroughly. I begged God for light, took our manuals in hand, examined everything strictly, compared the doctrines with the sacred Scriptures; and the more I examined and compared, the clearer it became to my mind, that the lodge and God's word contradict each other, even when they seem to agree, as, for example, in regard to the ten commandments. Even there, I learned to see that there was no agreement, farther than in the sound of words, and that the lodge denies the Lawgiver, the Triune God, and perverts the nature and true meaning of the ten commandments. In no place did the irreconcilable antagonism of the doctrine of the lodge to that of the Scriptures strike me more forcibly and convincingly, than in the doctrine of salvation. By this examination I have learned that it is literally true: the lodge teaches that we can be saved by our own virtues, while the sacred Scriptures teach we can be saved alone by faith in Jesus Christ. It became more and more clear to my mind, by this examination, that it was a grievous sin for me to remain longer in an association that teaches such grievous errors; and still I could not yet summon up courage to resolve': I will tell them that I withdraw from them. I wanted to come to you, was already near your house, but had no courage to come in and speak with you about the matter. I think shame held me back, for I well knew your opinion beforehand.

Ch. I should have been very glad had you come in. What such and similar battles with our evil hearts are, I know well enough from my own experience. You did not need to be ashamed.

E. Not being able, as yet, to come to the resolution to do what the word of God demands, and to which my conscience urged me, I prayed frequently and earnestly that our faithful God would grant me courage and strength. He has promised to hear prayer, and I received courage and joyfulness to form the resolution; so that I, after quiet deliberation, made up my mind to renounce the lodge. But I would first lay the whole matter before our pastor, and for that purpose called on him a short time ago. I first begged him to give me his opinion about the connection of a Christian with the lodge. This, of course, according to Scripture, could be no other than he gave it. He said, among other things: "A Christian, who believes in his Lord Jesus and *knows* the false doctrine of the lodge and its antagonism to the church, cannot possibly be a member of the lodge without denying Christ." When I told him I was convinced of it, and was now resolved to separate from the lodge, he praised God, and was heartily rejoiced. He added much more, and encouraged me to take this step courageously, in God's name. He referred me to the example of the Apostle Paul, who had also been in the fellowship of an unbelieving body, namely, the sect of the Pharisees, who also rejected Christ; but as soon as he had come to the knowledge of the truth, he had separated himself from them and had followed Christ alone. He also exhorted me, when I should announce my withdrawal from the lodge, to do it in a quiet, humble and gentle manner, and to tell the lodge members the plain truth, and give the real reason for my leaving. For, he said, in such a case it did not suffice that a Christian merely declare his withdrawal, but it was absolutely demanded that he should confess Christ and show that the teaching of the lodge most glaringly contradicts the word of God, and that on that account he withdrew, and, as a Christian, was bound to do so. Such testimony he thought could perhaps, sooner or later, produce good fruit. Finally, he admonished me, whenever I had an opportunity, to show all manner of kindness to the lodge members, the more so because these people usually imagine we hate them, and that this is the reason we withdraw from them. I should therefore prove by my acts, that instead of hating, I really loved them. Well, that I should have done of my own self; for God knows I love their persons and do not hate them. After our beloved pastor had wished me God's blessing upon my purpose, I left him joyfully and with a light heart. At the last meeting of the lodge I carried out my resolution and made known my withdrawal.

Ch. Now, praise and thanks be to God! But how was your resolution received?

E. I declared that I was bound by my conscience to announce my withdrawal, and then began to give the reasons for so doing, saying that the lodge teaches the direct opposite of what the sacred Scriptures teach. The lodge teaches, in all its books and publications, that man must make himself worthy of Heaven and gain it by his own virtues; the word of God, however, teaches that we can only be saved by grace, through Jesus Christ. This was clearly and plainly written, for example, Titus 3 : 5 : "Not by works of righteousness which we have done." And I was about to quote this passage, as well as some others, when the Noble Grand called me to order and said that anything like that was entirely out of place here. The doctrine of the Bible did not concern us as a lodge; we dare not dispute about religion here. This was a lodge meeting, and in it we dare only transact lodge business. I tried once more to gain the floor, and when I succeeded I said I had certainly the right to give my reasons for leaving the lodge, and would beg them to listen. This I was then permitted to do, with the remark to be brief. I then went on: "The lodge teaching directly contrary to the teachings of the Scriptures, I am, as a Christian, compelled to separate from it and declare my withdrawal. The lodge, for example, teaches that we are saved by works; the holy Scriptures, however, say we are saved by grace. I beg you not to think that this step is taken from ill will toward the members of the lodge." This declaration seemed to make a very different impression on the different members. Some looked at me with a compassionate shrug of the shoulders; others with doubtful, apparently sneering smiles; still others looked sullen, yea, angry. Several speakers now arose. What was said, I prefer to keep to myself. From some, it is true, I expected nothing else; from others I had hoped for something better. Ah, it makes me really sorry for the poor benighted souls! I heartily wish that many of them came to the knowledge of the truth.

Ch. I am rejoiced that you have taken this step. We will thank God heartily therefor; for it is not our merit, but entirely his grace, when we learn the truth. If we had not his blessed Word as a light unto our path, and did he not give us the grace of his Holy Spirit to enlighten our mind, we could never more attain to a saving knowledge. Neither will we forget to pray earnestly for those who are still under the pernicious influence of false doctrine and of unbelieving fellowship. We will pray in the words of that beautiful hymn:

> "Fill with the radiance of Thy grace
> The souls now lost in error's maze,
> And all, O Lord, whose secret minds
> Some dark delusion hurts and blinds.
> And all who else have strayed from Thee,
> O, gently seek! Thy healing be
> To every wounded conscience given,
> And let them also share Thy Heaven."

I also wish that it would please God to compensate you richly in earthly things for what you have lost by taking this step.

E. I believe the blessed God has done that long since. He has given us health, and preserved it until now, that we could earn our daily bread and something beside. He, who provides for the birds and clothes the lilies, will surely support and clothe us. The lost money is nothing but temporal blessing; not that I would by any means despise temporal blessings; they are also gifts of God's grace; but the spiritual blessings and gifts, such as forgiveness of sins, peace with God, joy in the Holy Ghost and everlasting salvation, are certainly a thousand times more valuable than all the goods of this earth. And surely Paul is not wrong when he says: "I count all things but loss for the excellency of the knowledge of Christ Jesus my Lord" (Phil. 3:8). It being a sin to remain any longer in the lodge, and I being in great danger of losing my salvation, and strengthening others in their error by my example, it was, according to God's word, my duty to take this step. I will joyfully bear the trifling loss of earthly things.

Ch. Blessed are we, when we are ready to leave all and to sacrifice everything, if Christ desires it of us, that we may confess and follow him.

E. When I look back upon my more than ten years' association with the lodge, it grieves me to the heart that I till now have lived in such blindness, approved of sins against God and his blessed word, and did not sooner come to the knowledge of the truth. May God in mercy forgive me. I did not, until lately, clearly see what a great sin it is for a Christian to unite with the lodge, nor how grievously the lodge sins by denying the true God and his word; yet I have, now and then, felt as if some things were not in order. To mention only one,—it never seemed right to me, that the lodge, which so frequently boasts of being a society for charitable purposes and mutual aid, did not render more assistance to the poor and weak outside of the order. I once endeavored to labor in that direction, and said, since persons with chronic diseases, old people and such as could not earn their own support, as our regulations and laws now are, could not be received as members, the lodge might grant them, of its own free will, a weekly assistance. But I did not succeed. It was answered that the resources of the lodge would not allow it; and yet we had many wealthy members, and some who had many thousands upon interest. That grieved me to the heart.

Ch. Yes, that is really so. The lodge sounds its trumpet loudly in praise of its deeds of charity, but, strictly considered, it only cares for itself. Egotism and self-interest are its governing motives. And yet nearly all the members of the lodge are so blinded, that they see neither the false doctrine nor the wrong doing. The lodge proves itself to be anti-christian in doctrine and practice. But, in spite of this, it endeavors to make the people believe that this order of Odd Fellows "*was instituted for the glory of God*"; that it is its duty "*to let the light of truth shine forth also in this country*"; that in the lodge, which is called "*the House of God*," "*Friendship, Love and Truth are practiced*" (See "Odd Fellow," August, 1870, p. 500 ff.). And yet, strictly speaking, the order has no truth, least of all, one which promotes "the glory of God." The members of the lodge call themselves "the people of God's pasture" and "the sheep of his hand" (Manual, p. 163), and assert that they will reform the world (Compare Man., pp. 113, 132 ff., 384; Pocket Comp., p. 111, 309 ff.). Yea, the lodge does not hesitate to act as if it were the Church of God, and to apply prophecies given to the Church to itself (Compare Man., p. 125, 134, &c.). What, in reality, is its position toward the church, with her Word and Sacraments, we see, for example, from the action of the Grand Lodge of West Virginia, which, at its Convention in April, 1870, approved of and confirmed the exclusion of two members of William

Toll Lodge, No. 6, because they belonged to a congregation which rejects the doctrines and principles of the order, and declared, on this occasion, that if a member of such a congregation united with the lodge, he should *immediately* withdraw from the congregation.* It does not stop to inquire whether it is a congregation's right or duty to reject their doctrine. Exalted above God's word and Church, it arbitrarily commands what seems good unto itself.

E. It is indeed a melancholy truth, that the lodge, with its doctrine and practice, stands in entire antagonism to the Church of Christ. It is true, his word is not recognized; they think nothing of it, and consider themselves far above it.

Ch. The Lord Jesus says (Matt. 7 : 16, 17): "Ye shall know them by their fruits. Do men gather grapes of thorns or figs of thistles? Even so every good tree bringeth forth good fruit; but a corrupt tree bringeth forth evil fruit." The worst of all the "evil fruits" which this order brings forth, is its false doctrine. First of all, and the most terrible of all maxims, is, that not the sacred Scriptures, but conscience, perverted by sin and ungoverned by the word of God, is the highest "authority," the only rule and standard in matters of religion and faith. From this follow, and must necessarily follow, all other fundamental errors, such as: the false doctrine of God and the denial of the holy Trinity; the false doctrine of adoption by God, of salvation and of prayer. From these false doctrines proceed, then, the evil fruits in practical life, such as: contempt of God's word, of the Church and the Sacraments; hatred toward the true children of God; egotism and selfishness; the extolling of selfish works as deeds of charity and good works, which merit heaven; the approval, yea encouragement and defence of the most frightful perjury, and the like.

---

* See "Heart and Hand," Aug. 13th, 1870.

E. Praise and thanks be to our faithful God that he has brought me out of darkness and uncertainty to the true knowledge, and has saved me from this corrupt association. May God graciously save many more, yea, if it were possible, all who are still imprisoned in this darkness, and bring them to the light of life.

Ch. That is also my desire and prayer. May the Lord, our God, grant his "Yea" and "Amen" thereto!

APPENDIX.

A Brief Sketch of the Order of Odd Fellows,

DRAWN FROM THEIR OWN PUBLICATIONS.

I.—ANTIQUITY OF THE ORDER.

Almost without exception, the members of secret societies seek to represent their order as of ancient origin. Particularly is this the case with Free Masons and Odd Fellows. They take pains to prove that their order dates back to the Roman Emperor Nero, to Solomon, yea even to Adam. In the Grand Lodge of the United States there is "an emblem representing Adam laying the foundation-stone of the order" (Manual, p. 24). That this is ridiculous, every Christian must see at the first glance. Were it true that the lodge reached back as far as Solomon or Adam, we would willingly leave them this more than doubtful honor; but it is by no means true. But why is it that so many members of the lodge take pains to spread the opinion that their order is of so ancient origin? No doubt in order by its great age to create a great impression, to make it appear as if their order was some old, venerable institution, and because venerable, doubtless also something good. To this end, they do not hesitate to represent John the Baptist, John the Evangelist, Solomon, Moses, Aaron and Adam as Free Masons or Odd Fellows.

That the Odd Fellows, in proving the antiquity of their order, must contradict themselves in the most ridiculous manner, is evident, because not the slightest *real* proof of great age can be adduced from history; and that for the very simple reason that in old times there was no order of Odd Fellows. In the Improved Manual for Odd Fellows, by A. B. Grosh, we read, on page 25, that all the traditions of the origin of the order under Adam, Moses and Aaron, during the Babylonish captivity and the Roman Emperors, "and other baseless and silly stories, ... have been utterly discarded as without proof and absurd, by the Grand Lodge of the United States," and that many years ago. Notwithstanding, the "Pocket-Book of the Odd Fellows," of 1868, takes pains, in all earnestness, to make the members believe that the order is no doubt of very ancient origin. We read (p. 14 ff.) as follows: "Some have dated it (the order) as far back as Adam, who was said to have laid the foundation-stone of the order. Others intimate that it existed among the ancient Jewish priesthood, under the lead of Moses and Aaron. One says that it was organized in A. D. 55, among the Roman soldiers, and that its present name was suggested by Cæsar, who called the brethren *Odd Fellows* because they recognized each other by day and by night. It has been proved* that the order was established in the Spanish dominions in the fifth century, and that it was also introduced into Portugal in the sixth century, by King Henry; that in the twelfth century it was established in France, and afterward in England, by John De Neville, attended by five

---

* Where is this proof to be found?

knights from France, who formed a 'Loyal Grand Lodge of Honor" in London, that existed until the eighteenth century, during the reign of George III, when a part of them began to form a society of their own, a portion of which remains up to the present day; that the lodges which originated from these several organizations are numerous throughout the world, and have been called, at different periods, 'Loyal Ancient Odd Fellows,' 'Union Odd Fellows' and 'Manchester Union Odd Fellows.'"
"*I see no good reason,*" the author of the book says further, "*why these historical accounts of the order should be disputed,* and am inclined, therefore, to believe that it emanated from some of the original sources above named." The same inextricable contradiction is also to be found in the periodicals of the order; for example, in the paper bearing the title, "The Odd Fellow." In the July number, of 1870, page 436, the traditions of the great age of the Odd Fellows, their existence in the times of Moses, Solomon and the Roman emperors are called "baseless" and "ridiculous assertions." On page 439, however, the writer of an article seeks to prove that the origin or the foundation of the order dates back to the reign of the Emperor Nero, because it was founded in the year 55 after Christ, by Roman soldiers. At that time they called the members of this society Fellow-citizens. The name which they bear to-day was given them twenty-four years after the foundation of the order by the Emperor Titus. With such contradictory nonsense and fabricated history, men are fooled by those who have "Truth" for their motto and who pretend that lies are banished from their midst.

The order is of very recent origin, as has frequently been proved by history, and not yet been refuted; among others, by Prof. Hengstenberg, in his book, "Freemasonry and the Evangelical Pastoral Office," Berlin, 1854. The Freemasonry of to-day was fabricated in the year 1717, on the 24th of June, in London, England, and so came into existence. Previous to that time there never were such Free Mason lodges. It is true there were Masons' guilds at an earlier date, as also the other crafts had their guilds and associations, and some have them still. Those Masons' guilds and unions had nothing in common with our Free Masons of to-day. The Masons' associations previous to 1717 were governed by the Word of God, and exercised Christian discipline. No one was admitted into these associations who despised God's word or the holy sacraments; the masters and overseers guarded Christian order and required a godly life.

In the year 1717 the present Freemasonry was "invented," which, unlike the Masons of old and their guilds, labors with the trowel and hammer, but uses them in plays and fooleries. Neither is it the aim of this society of Free Masons to improve and perfect themselves in the art of architecture, which was one of the chief objects of the ancient guild of Masons; but their aim was to bring men, who until then had believed in and lived according to God's word, another light, namely, that natural religion which every one has by nature, even from his birth, and to convince them that it is the one right and true religion. Thereby they did then and do now design to "enlighten" the spirit of man, and of course bring all those, who suffer themselves to be thus "enlightened," away from the light of God's word into the thick darkness of their own blinded hearts.

That the Freemasonry of to-day is not older, we can learn from the book of R. Clemen, "The Origin, Development and Signification of Secret Societies," Columbus, Ohio, 1860. The author is a genuine Free Mason and Odd Fellow, which he proves, among other things, by what he says on page 61: Many of the ancients understood the birth of God's Son literally, took the type for the idea concealed in the type, and accordingly those of modern times believe also in a literal sense in the Son of God. And, in order to prevent this belief, that is contradictory to the very Being of God, from going to decay, they take the greatest pains to pervert the order of nature, and over and again to prove that and how God could have a Son. And in the conclusion of his book, after endeavoring to sully the faithful servants of Christ plentifully with his venom, and elevating and praising the apostates (provided they had become members of the lodge), he declares (p. 134): "Hell is only for those who invented it." Well, this Mr. Clemen himself acknowledges that the Freemasonry of to-day is no older (p. 76). To be sure he takes pains to prove an affinity of principle and spirit with the earlier Masonic guilds, in which he of course does not succeed, and never will, because those Masonic guilds stood upon the foundation of God's Word and the Christian Church; the present Freemasons, however, on the foundation of a mongrel religion of reason.

This order of Free Masons, like all other weeds, is fruitful, and is the mother of many other secret societies. Our Odd Fellow order undoubtedly springs from it, as its doctrines prove, which essentially coincide with those of the order of Free Masons, just as its constitution is essentially the same. An "ex-master" of the Odd Fellows, L. Meyer, tells the same thing in the "Odd Fellow" of November, 1870, page 690. Among other things, he says: "In the Masonic alliance we find . . . the beginning of our order." And further: "The foundation of our order is to be looked for in the last ten years of the last century." But not even the slightest proof, which will bear the test, has hitherto been given, that this order was founded before 1800. We find the first historical proof of its existence in England in the year 1809. At this time we find the members of the order frequently assembled in houses of doubtful reputation, making merry over the mug of beer and other worldly amusements. In the year 1813 several lodges separated from them and formed a union of their own, under the name of "Independent Order of Odd Fellows." As this branch of the Odd Fellows more or less did away with the beer drinking at their lodge meetings, and, what certainly was the main point, assisted its members more liberally in case of sickness, it spread very quickly, which is not to be wondered at when we remember that it was a time barren and gloomy as regards Christian faith and activity. From this branch of the order afterwards originated other independent associations, among others the "Manchester Unity," from which the lodge members in this country count their origin.

Thomas Wildey, a blacksmith, immigrated in the year 1817 from England, and founded the order here in 1819, which remained in connection with the order in England until the year 1843. It then deemed itself strong enough to be self-reliant, and therefore separated from the order in England, notwithstanding the latter had treated the Odd Fellows in this country very liberally, had given them charters and their own jurisdiction. They did not like, however, to be subject any longer to any other authority, which could throw hindrances in the way of their rule and ambition; and so the Grand Lodge of the United States declared itself "*the only Fountain and Depository of Independent Oddfellowship on the globe*" (Manual, p. 55). In this manner the alliance was cut off, and brotherly love came to an end. Indeed the usurped authority went so far in proscribing all the much vaunted love for the mother lodge in England, that to this day it forbids its members to unite with a lodge of the "Manchester Unity," under pain of expulsion.* And since the Grand Lodge of the United States has proclaimed itself to be "the only fountain of Independent Odd Fellowship on the globe," it recognizes no other order of Odd Fellows, and therefore neither card nor any other document from the Manchester Unity is considered valid by it. If the Manchester Unity wishes to be acknowledged, it must bow before its own revolutionary child, and beg from the same permission for its existence, in the form of a charter.

---

* See Digest, p. 236 ff.

Is it still asked, why these and other secret societies were founded at all, we reply, with the "Odd Fellow," without satisfactorily answering the question, that: "*The doubter in the circle of the brethren . . . can express himself more freely*" ("O. F.," Nov., 1870, p. 690), and that "*free religious views might develop themselves*" ("O. F.," July, 1871, p. 56). The religious views, or, better, the Christian doctrines of the sacred Scriptures, were not free enough for these people; the doctrine of repentance and faith did not please them; to be saved by grace, they did not like; and on that account, as the Odd Fellows themselves say, secret societies were established.

II.—GOVERNMENT.

1.—EXTERNAL DIVISION.

The order consists of two departments, namely, Lodges and Encampments.

(A)—LODGES.

(*a*). *Subordinate Lodges.*—Subordinate Lodges are those which stand under the jurisdiction of a State Grand Lodge, or, in case none such exists in the respective States, under the immediate jurisdiction of the Grand Lodge of the United States. When five lodge members are found in a place where there is no lodge or where, according to their opinion, there are too few lodges, they can apply to the Grand Lodge of the State, or, in case none such exists, to the Grand Lodge of the United States, for a charter, and if this is granted, they can found a new lodge. The petitioners dare, however, never neglect to enclose the charter, fee, which is usually thirty dollars. That is the main point ; for, without respectable payment, the Grand Lodge concerned will move neither hand nor foot, neither pencil nor pen, and still less will it without money grant permission to a number of persons to assent to its false doctrines and to assume the obligation to be obedient to it. The form of such a petition, as determined by law, is the following (see Digest, p. 419; Pocket Comp., p. 274):

"To the Grand Sire, Officers and Members of the Grand Lodge of the United States: The petition of the undersigned, holding withdrawal cards from lodges legally recognized by your R. W. body, respectfully represents that it would be consistent with the advantages of the order, to establish a Subordinate Lodge, to be located at ———, in the State of ———. Wherefore your petitioners pray that a Warrant may duly issue, in pursuance of the laws of your R. W. body."

As soon as the petition, with the handsome sum of money, has arrived, for which not one drop of sweat has been shed, the "R. W. Grand Lodge" generally condescends most graciously to grant the request. The form in which it is given is the following (see Digest, p. 421 ff.; Pocket Comp., p. 275 ff.):

"I, Most Worthy Grand Sire of the Grand Lodge of the Independent Order of Odd Fellows of the United States of America and the jurisdiction of the Order thereunto belonging:

"*Friendship, Love and Truth.*

"Know ye, that, by virtue of the powers in me vested, I do hereby authorize and empower our trusty and well-beloved brethren, ——— ———, and their successors, duly and legally elected, to constitute a lodge in the ——— of ——— and State of ———, to be known and hailed by the title of ———. And I do further authorize and empower our said trusty and well-beloved brethren and their successors to admit and make Odd Fellows according to the ancient usages and customs of the Order, and not contrarywise; with full power and authority to hear and determine all and singular matters and things relating to the Order within the jurisdiction of the said lodge, according to the rules and regulations of the Grand Lodge of the United States. Provided, always, that the said above-named brethren and their successors *pay due respect* to the Grand Lodge of the United States and the ordinances thereof; otherwise this Dispensation to be of no force or effect

'Given under my hand and the seal of the Grand Lodge of the United States, at the city of Baltimore," &c.

After the reception of such a "charter," the new lodge is "instituted" or "opened" with all manner of pomp and pageantry, by the respective Grand Lodges, and their elected officers, namely, Noble Grand, Vice Grand, one or two Secretaries and a Treasurer, are installed. This installation may be performed by the "Most Worthy Grand Master" in his own proper person, or by a Deputy. Of course the new lodge must pay all the traveling expenses, and so forth. In order to give an insight into the fooleries, buffooneries and lying honorary titles, and at the same time to become acquainted with the ungodly straight-jacket into which the Grand Lodge puts every subordinate lodge and every member of the order, without previously affording them opportunity for examination and reflection, we give such a disgusting ceremonial of the "installation of the officers of the subordinate lodges," from the Digest, page 434 ff., and Pocket Comp., page 252 ff. But it must not be forgotten, that this is the form used at *public* installations. What takes place at *secret* installations, behind closed doors, is not made known to any "profane" person. Nevertheless, this formula suffices perfectly. It runs as follows:

"All the ordinary ceremonies of the lodge being suspended, the inner door being opened wide, and the officers in their respective stations, the Grand Marshal, having a white baton, trimmed with scarlet, approaches, and the following conversation ensues:

"*Grand Marshal.* Worthy Guardian, inform the Noble Grand

that the Grand Marshal of the R. W. Grand Lodge of —— demands admission.

"*Inside Guardian.* Noble Grand, the W. Grand Marshal of the —— is without, and demands admission.

"*Noble Grand.* You will admit him.

"*Inside Guardian.* You have liberty to enter.

"The Grand Marshal passes to the center of the lodge, facing the Noble Grand, whom he salutes with the baton.

"*Grand Marshal.* Worthy Noble Grand, I am instructed, by the M. W. Grand Master of the R. W. Grand Lodge of the ——, to ascertain whether the charter (or dispensation) of this lodge is in the hall; whether the dues of this Lodge have been paid, and, if not, to request that they shall be placed in my hands;* to ask if the officers have been elected for the ensuing term; if they are free from all charges, pecuniary or otherwise, upon your lodge-books; and whether you are now ready to proceed with the ceremony of installation?

"*Noble Grand.* Worthy Grand Marshal, the charter of this Lodge is in the lodge-room, and in my keeping. The Treasurer will pay over to you the dues of the Lodge, or show you the Grand Secretary's receipt for the same. The officers for the ensuing term have been elected; they each and all stand free from all charges upon our lodge-books. You will please inform the M. W. Grand Master that we are prepared for installation, and await his pleasure.

"After receiving the dues, the Grand Marshal again salutes the Noble Grand and retires. The procession being formed, the grand officers approach the door.

"*Grand Marshal.* The Grand Lodge of the Independent Order of Odd Fellows of ——.

"*Inside Guardian.* Noble Grand, the Grand Lodge.

---

* The Grand Marshal knew all this beforehand.

"*Noble Grand.* In the name of Friendship, Love and Truth, admit them.

"They enter and pass to the center of the hall. The lodge rises. The Grand Master steps in front.

"*Grand Master.* Noble Grand, by authority of the R. W. Grand Lodge of ——, we appear here this evening for the purpose of installing into their respective chairs the officers of this lodge. You will please direct your officers to surrender their respective chairs to the grand officers in attendance, and you will now please take your seat as Sitting Past Grand of this lodge for the current term.

"*Noble Grand.* Officers of —— Lodge, you will surrender your chairs to the officers of the R. W. Grand Lodge of ——.

"The Grand Master will take the Noble Grand's chair, the Grand Warden will take the Vice Grand's, the Grand Secretary will take the Secretary's, and the Grand Treasurer will take the Treasurer's chair.

"*Grand Master.* My brethren, you will please be seated. Worthy Grand Marshal, you will retire with the officers elect for examination. It is unnecessary for me to remind you that that duty should be faithfully performed.

"After the examination of the candidates, the Grand Marsha will announce, through the Grand Guardian:

"The Grand Marshal, with the officers elect for installation.

"The Grand Marshal and officers elect will enter in procession, the lodge remaining seated. Each of the officers may be supported by two who have passed the same office, and will form a line on the left of the Noble Grand's chair. During the march into the lodge, the following may be sung:

"INSTALLATION ODE.

"Come, let us swell the joyful note,
And hail the chosen band,
Who, in compliance with our vote,
To-night before us stand.

Our Noble and Vice Grand will now
  To seats of honor move,
And bear the ensign on their brow
  Of Friendship, Truth and Love.

"Hail! all our officers elect,
  Of high and low degree,
Hail! each with due and kind respect
  Whate'er his station be.
We place reliance in their zeal,
  That they will worthy prove,
And stamp their actions with the seal
  Of Friendship, Truth and Love.

"*Grand Marshal.* M. W. Grand Master, I present to you for installation our worthy brother (A. B.), whom the brethren of this lodge have elected Noble Grand for the present term.

"*Grand Master.* (To the Noble Grand elect.) Brother, do you accept of the office to which you have been elected?

Noble Grand elect. I do.

"*Grand Master.* (To the lodge.) Brethren, are you content with the choice you have made of Noble Grand?

"*Answer* (usually in the affirmative).

"Should any objection be expressed, the Grand Master, if the installation be in public, will recall the officers to their respective chairs, and, with the grand officers, will retire. If the installation be in private, it will be the duty of the Grand Master to examine its nature; and if it should appear that the election has been effected by irregular or illegal means, the Grand Master shall order a new election to take place at that time, which he shall conduct, and the person then elected, if qualified, shall be installed. These directions apply to all the officers.

"*Grand Master.* M. W. Grand Marshal, have you examined the Noble Grand elect, to ascertain whether he is sufficiently acquainted with the various lectures and instructions to enable him to deliver them according to his office? Have you ascertained whether he has rendered sufficient previous service in office, and is free from all charges on the books of this lodge, of whatsoever kind?

"*Grand Marshal.* I have, M. W. Grand Master, and find the brother competent and eligible to fill the honorable station to which he has been elected by the brothers of this lodge.

"*Grand Master.* Noble Grand elect, will you promise to submit to your charges; to be obedient to the mandates of the Grand Lodge of the ———; to support the regulations of our order; to act with justice toward all brothers, as is the duty of a Noble Grand?

"*Noble Grand elect.* I will.

"*Grand Master.* Your apparent willingness to conform to the charges and regulations of our order, the proficiency you have made therein, your moral standing, your freedom from indebtedness to the lodge, and the voice of a majority thereof, entitle you to be now installed into the office of Noble Grand of this lodge. You will, therefore, place your right hand upon your left breast, and repeat after me:

"*Noble Grand's O. B. N.* (Signifies *Oath.* The Author.*)— In the presence of the members of the order here assembled, I, ———, do promise, declare, and say, that I will perform the duties of Noble Grand of this lodge until the end of the present term; and will support, maintain and abide by the Constitution, By-Laws, Rules and Regulations of the Grand Lodge of the Independent Order of Odd Fellows of the ———, as well as the Constitution and By-Laws of this Lodge. I furthermore promise, that I will not give the means whereby to gain admission, to any person except a member of this Lodge, in good standing. I will, to the utmost of my power, enforce the laws, and preserve order and decorum in the Lodge. I will judge of every transaction that comes

---

* Compare Digest, p. 528. Index Article: Oath.

before me without prejudice or partiality ; see that the obligations to candidates for membership are legally administered; and, should the Grand Lodge direct, I will deliver the Warrant or Dispensation of this Lodge to the Grand Master. All this I promise to fulfill, unless prevented by sickness, or some other unavoidable occurrence. To the performance of all which I pledge my most sacred honor.

"*Grand Master.* W. Grand Marshal, you will proceed to nvest the Noble Grand in the regalia of his office.

"*Grand Marshal.* By command of the M. W. Grand Master, I invest you with this collar, jewel, and other regalia, which are emblems of your office.

"*Grand Master.* Noble Grand, you will receive from us the Constitution and By-Laws of your Lodge; you are to take them for your guide, and cause them to be frequently read in your Lodge. You will please be seated at our right hand.

,,*Grand Marshal.* M. W. Grand Master, I present to you, for installation, our worthy brother (C. D), whom the brethren of this Lodge have elected Vice Grand for the present term.

"*Grand Master.* Brother, do you accept the office to which you have been elected?

"*Vice Grand elect.* I do.

"*Grand Master.* Brethren of the Lodge, are you content in the choice you have made of Vice Grand?

"*Answer.* (*As in case of Noble Grand.*)

"*Grand Master.* W. Grand Marshal, have you examined the Vice Grand elect, to ascertain whether he is sufficiently acquainted with the various lectures and instructions to enable him to assist in delivering them according to his office? Have you ascertained whether he has rendered sufficient previous service in office, and is free from all charges on the books of this Lodge, of whatsoever kind?

"*Grand Marshal.* I have, M. W. Grand Master, and find the

brother competent and eligible to fill the honorable station to which he has been elected by the brothers of this Lodge.

"*Grand Master.* Vice Grand elect, will you promise to yield a like obedience to your charges and the mandates of the R. W. Grand Lodge, as the Noble Grand; to assist him in the execution of his office; to use your efforts in promoting the harmony and welfare of the Lodge, and to increase love among your brethren?

"*Vice Grand elect.* I will.

"*Grand Master.* In consequence of your avowed willingness to enter upon and perform the duties of Vice Grand of this Lodge, you will now proceed with our W. Grand Marshal to the chair of your office, where you will be installed. W. Grand Marshal, you will present the Vice Grand elect to our R. W. Grand Warden for obligation.

"*Grand Marshal.* R. W. Grand Warden, by command of our M. W. Grand Master, I present you brother (C. D.), the Vice Grand elect, for obligation.

"*Grand Warden.* Vice Grand elect, you will please place your right hand upon your left breast, and repeat after me:

"*Vice Grands O. B. N.* (*Oath.* The Author.)—In the presence of the members of the order now assembled," and so forth.

(Essentially the same oath as that of the Noble Grand. Author.)

"*Grand Master.* W. Grand Marshal, you will proceed to invest the Vice Grand with the regalia of his office.

"*Grand Marshal.* By command of the M. W. Grand Master, I invest you with the badges of your office. In receiving them, you will not cease to remember that the preference of the Lodge has placed them upon you, in the full confidence that, while you wear them, their purity shall not be blemished.

"*Grand Warden.* Vice Grand, I present to you a copy of the Constitution and By-Laws of your Lodge, which you will make your study, in order that you may assist the Noble Grand in the performance of his duties; and this gavil, which indicates that you are to assist him in the exercise of his authority. You will now take your seat as Vice Grand of this Lodge for the present term."

In like manner are then the Recording Secretary, the Permanent Secretary, and the Treasurer, "presented," sworn in, and invested with the appointed regalia (better speaking; mummeries) for the respective offices. After, then, by "command" of the "M. W. Grand Master," the "Noble Grand" has appointed his other officers (the whole number of officers in a lodge is but seventeen), the "M. W. Grand Master turns again to the "Noble Grand" with the following words:

"Noble Grand, previous to delivering into your keeping the charter and books pertaining to your office, it is necessary that you should enter with us into another obligation. Place yourself in the attitude in which you were last obligated, and repeat:

"I, Noble Grand, do, in the presence of these brethren, most sincerely promise and declare, that I will neither print nor write, nor cause to be printed or written, any part or parts of the secret work of Oddfellowship; nor will I, in the presence of any person, either read or rehearse, or cause to be understood by any means, any part or parts of it, except in the presence of brothers duly qualified to receive the same in legal form. Nor will I, at any time, permit these books to be taken from my keeping, by any person or persons, excepting those subordinate officers whose various charges shall have obligated them to return to me such printed or written part or parts as were delivered to them, without having made, themselves, or permitted any others to make, any extracts, or take any copies therefrom; and I will use every effort to effect the return of those books, or printed or written parts of them, as soon as the purpose for which they were obtained from me has been accomplished. And I do furthermore promise and declare, that I will deliver these books to no person or persons, excepting the M. W. Grand Master, or his Deputy, or to a committee from the Grand Lodge, and the Noble Grand who shall have been elected to succeed me. To the performance of all which I pledge my most sacred honor."

It is therefore not enough that the Noble Grand swears once, he must swear twice before taking possession of his "office." That done, the "M. W. Grand Master" confidently delivers the books and writings into his hands, those which even the "profane" may read, as well as those which dare not be polluted by the hands of the unclean.

After this terribly tedious ceremony follows a long string of charges, addressed to each officer separately, the main substance of which is always a charge to obedience, which is just as tedious, and which we also rather omit. After this lengthy, repulsive ceremony, during which some cannot refrain from laughter, and others from sleep, follows the solemn conclusion, when the Grand Marshal takes the floor, and with a certain omnipotence and with raised voice, says:

"And now, by command of the M. W. Grand Master, and in the name and by the authority of the Right Worthy Grand Lodge of ——, of the Independent Order of Odd Fellows, I do declare the officers of —— Lodge, No. ——, installed into their respective offices for the current term, in —— form."

The brethren answer: "So be it."

Having, then, for this time, sufficiently worthied each other, and having all (at least the officers) descended beneath the name of a Christian and the dignity of men; having reverenced a Grand Man, "mostly and very highly"; having debased themselves as his slaves, his obedient servants and sycophants, it will be difficult for them ever again to attain to the dignity of men, and still more so to attain to the dignity of Christians.

That the audience now heartily rejoices at last to have this tedious comedy ended, and disperses in a very good humor, is readily to be understood, the more so, as in most cases the accumulated "thirst" claims its due. However, the lodge is formed and established, and every one who desires to be a servant of men can, by paying the fee for proposal, usually three dollars, be proposed for admission.*

In every subordinate lodge, the Noble Grand exercises the government. Every one who does not obey his word, is immediately punished, and has either to pay down a fine or must allow himself to enjoy the honor of being suspended or put out of doors.

No one is allowed to speak in the lodge, or to vote, who does not appear in his proper regalia. At the election of officers, no one can vote who owes the lodge anything, should it only be five cents. If any one is in arrears with his dues for three months, he can only attend the weekly meetings of the lodge by special permission of the "Noble Grand"; if he does not soon pay, he will be suspended or stricken from the roll.

(*b*). *The State Grand Lodges.*†—These assemble annually or semi-annually, and are composed of all the Past Grands. As, however, the lodge members of the first degrees are still groping too much in the dark, and the light of the lodge has not been sufficiently shed upon them; therefore the representatives can under no condition be others than Past Grands. These together form the Grand Lodge of the State. The elected officers of a Grand Lodge are: "M. W. Grand Master, R. W. Deputy Grand Master, R. W. Grand Warden, R. W. Grand Secretary, R. W. Grand Treasurer, who are elected annually; and R. W. Grand Representative, or Representatives, elected biennially." To these are added a host

---

* Some of the chief conditions for reception are, that the candidate be a free, white man, of good moral character, and not under twenty-one years of age; that he believe in a "Supreme Being, the Creator and Preserver of the Universe"; that he be healthy, can support himself, &c.

† According to the report of 1873, more than forty State Grand Lodges belong to the Grand Lodge of the United States.

of other "worthy" officers who are appointed by the M. W. Grand Master, among which the "W. Grand Chaplain" and the "Inside and Outside Guardians," "with drawn sword," must not be wanting

If in a State or Territory there is no Grand Lodge in existence, three or more lodges are permitted,* if they have seven Past Grands, to petition the Grand Lodge of the United States for permission to establish a State Grand Lodge; that is, if they are right humble, and promise perfect obedience, in every respect, to the Grand Lodge of the United States (G. L. U. S.), and do not forget to enclose the necessary fee, thirty dollars; for only under these conditions will the G. L U. S. take their petition in o consideration. For brevity's sake, we omit the form of this petition, as well as the form of the charter. They are essentially the same as with the subordinate lodge. The main point of such a charter, which the Right Worthy or Most Worthy Grand Sire graciously vouchsafes to grant, is always the demand for strict obedience and that of "due respect to the Grand Lodge of the United States and the ordinances thereof" (Pocket Comp., p. 200; Digest, p. 422). After such a charter has been granted (which usually is given), the Grand Lodge is most solemnly "organized" or "established" by the "Most Worthy Grand Sire," or his deputy with much pomp and parade. Such a State Grand Lodge has the jurisdiction over all the lodges of the respective State. No lodge of the "Independent order of Odd Fellows" (I. O. O. F.) can be established in the State without its permission, and without having paid for it And, should it occur to any lodge not to render prompt obedience, or to wish to obey God rather than man, it would forthwith be suspended, and the Grand Lodge would confiscate all the property, which the members have often acquired with their hard-earned money.† And, as the subordinate lodges (S. L.) are bound

---

* The Manual says ten lodges are requisite (p. 419).
† See, for example, Manual, p. 439 ff.

to the strictest obedience to the State Grand Lodge (S. G. L.); so are these obligated to pay the strictest obedience to the Grand Lodge of the United States.

(c). *The Grand Lodge of the United States (G. L. U. S.).**— "The highest authority and judicatory of the order. It 'possesses original and exclusive jurisdiction,' and is the source of all true and legitimate authority in Oddfellowship in the United States of America." It is the ultimate tribunal to which all matters of general importance to the State, District and Territorial Grand Lodges and Encampments are to be referred, and "its decisions thereon shall be final and conclusive." "To it belongs the power to control and regulate the work of the order, and the several degrees belonging thereto, and to fix and determine the customs and usages in regard to all things which pertain to Oddfellowship. It has inherent power to establish lodges or encampments in foreign countries where no Grand Lodge or Grand Encampment exists." "It supplies the A. T. P. W. (the yearly traveling pass-word) to all grand bodies in its jurisdiction" (Manual, p. 441 ff.; Digest, p. 159). It consists of the representatives of all the State Grand Lodges and its own officers. The officers are: "The Most Worthy Grand Sire, Right W. Deputy Grand Sire, R. W. Grand Corresponding and Recording Secretary, and R. W. Grand Treasurer," who are chosen biennially. To these are added a number of "right worthy" officers appointed by the "Most Worthy Grand Sire," among which a "Grand Chaplain" and a "Grand Guardian" dare not be wanting. The representatives are elected by the State Grand Lodges and Grand Encampments, *not by the members of the subordinate lodges.* For every 1000 members which a State Grand Lodge has in its subordinate lodges, the G. L. U. S. allows one vote or representative; but not with-

---

* It "was incorporated as such in the year 1841, by the Legislature of Maryland. Pocket Comp., p. 210.

out payment and gratis. For every representative the State Grand Lodge has to pay annually seventy-five dollars in cash, without reckoning the other contributions. A State Lodge cannot send more than two representatives. In order to be qualified to become a so-called Grand Representative, much is required; he must not only have been a Noble Grand, have received all the lodge and encampment degrees, but must also have been Grand Master of a State Grand Lodge*; all others are not yet sufficiently enlightened by the great light of the lodge to fill such an office.

This Grand Lodge of the United States assembles annually, and governs with sovereign power, not only in the United States, but also in Canada, Australia, South America, Germany, the Sandwich Islands, West Indies, and who knows where all else. To be sure, up to present date it only governs the lodges and encampments in those countries; but certainly we will not miss the mark by assuming that they, like the Jesuits, are hoping for better times. Should some State Grand Lodge presume not to obey it at a word, it would immediately be suspended and its property confiscated by the G. L. U. S. (Digest, p. 159).

The Apostle Paul admonishes us: "Be not ye the servants of men." Every Odd Fellow delivers himself to a triple bondage to men, without reckoning his bondage to the Prince of Darkness; in the first place, he is the slave of his Noble Grand; secondly, slave of his Grand Lodge; and thirdly, slave of the G. L. U. S. And this bondage is so great that, for instance, even his freedom of speech is taken from him, and he suffers himself quietly to be

---

* See Man., p. 443, In Digest, p. 193, 474, it is not demanded from a Grand Representative that he must have been Grand Master of a State Grand Lodge. This contradiction is perhaps explained by the fact that the law book holds more to theory, the Manual, however, more to the practice. It is a general custom to elect none but Past Grand Masters of the State Grand Lodges as Grand Representatives.

robbed of it. In the "standing resolutions of the Grand Lodge of Wisconsin" it is said, for example (§ 5) : "The officers and members of the subordinate lodges, which work under the jurisdiction of this Grand Lodge, are and shall be hereby admonished, not to engage in any controversy through the public press, nor to publish anything in connection with the order in the form of reports or speeches, without special permission from this Grand Lodge." And every member of the lodge willingly submits to this. They are enchained, by all manner of trickery, in iron chains and bonds, and submit to it all. And indeed it requires much before lodge members gain courage enough to let all their money and other lodge property go, in order to free themselves from these bonds and this servitude. It does not occur very frequently that members withdraw, but it is one of the greatest rarities that one leaves them on account of their blasphemous and pernicious doctrines.

(B)—The Encampment.

The Encampment Branch, or the "Patriarchal Branch," is usually held in higher estimation than the lodge, and that of right, because the light of the lodge shines in this considerably brighter. "Sublime degrees," "higher instructions" are imparted therein. "The lodge is of the civic type; the Encampment is of the military, but patriarchal, and therefore pastoral" (Manual, p. 354 ff.). "Though teaching peaceful lessons, the Encampment assumes military forms" (p. 360).

(a) *Subordinate Encampment.*—If a member of the lodge has received the five degrees, and is in "good standing," that is, if he has paid all dues of the lodge and there is no charge against him, he can become a member of an Encampment, but not without paying at least twelve to twenty dollars entrance fee. He must, however, continue to be a member of the lodge, in "good standing," so long as he wishes to remain a member of the Encampment. As such, he must of course pay double, namely, to the Lodge and to the Encampment.

The Encampment has its own constitution. The members meet usually every two weeks, and owe obedience to the State Grand Encampment. In case of disobedience, the Subordinate Encampment is suspended or excommunicated, and all the property, books, funds, &c., are confiscated by the Grand Encampment of the State;* indeed it can do so without previously instituting an investigation.

In a place where no Encampment exists, seven patriarchs (members of an Encampment), who have received the three "sublime degrees" of the Encampment, by sending the necessary fee, can apply for a charter from the Grand Encampment of the State, or, if none such exists, to the Grand Lodge of the United States; and, if granted, a new Encampment is organized, with all the prescribed ceremonies.† The officers of an Encampment, to be elected, are: a Chief Patriarch, a High Priest, a Senior Warden, a Scribe, a Treasurer, a Junior Warden: to these are added a host of appointed officers, as "Watches," "Sentinels," &c.

(b). *Grand Encampment.*—When no Grand Encampment is in existence in a State, five Subordinate Encampments, if they have seven Past Chief Patriarchs and send the Grand Lodge of the United States thirty dollars, can petition the same for a charter, and when this is granted, can establish a new Grand Encampment, with all manner of pomp (See Digest, p. 148 ff.). The same consists of all the past "Chief Patriarchs," and in

---

* See Digest, p. 154; Constitution of Grand Encampment of Wisconsin, Art. I, By-Laws, Art. II.

† We pass over the buffooneries of the establishment of a new Encampment and the installation of the officers. With insignificant changes, they are the same disgusting ceremonies, as with the lodge and its officers.

some States also of the past "High Priests." It has the jurisdiction over all the Encampments of the respective State; also permission, for every thousand members of its Subordinate Encampments, to send one representative to the Grand Lodge of the United States, provided it has not neglected to send, besides the other dues, seventy-five dollars for each representative.

The officers of a Grand Encampment, to be elected, are: "Most Worthy Grand Patriarch," "M. E. Grand High Priest, R. W. Grand Senior Warden, R. W. Grand Junior Warden, R. W. Grand Scribe," &c., in addition to which a number of "R. W. Grand Officers" are appointed, among which the "Watches" are never missing. The Grand Encampments* meet annually or semi-annually (in case no extra session is called together by the "M. W. Patriarch"), usually at the same time and place with the State Grand Lodge.

There is no separate Grand Encampment of the United States; it is combined with the Grand Lodge of the United States, which includes all the lodges and encampments. For this reason, all the representatives to the same must have taken all the degrees of the encampments. The State Grand Encampments are all responsible to the Grand Lodge of the United States, and should any Grand Encampment desire to set up its own authority, and not obediently to bend its neck under the iron yoke of the G. L. U. S., it would immediately be suspended or expelled, and all its property confiscated. (Digest, p. 159; Constitution of the G. Lodge U. S., Art. 1, 3.)

---

* To avoid conflict between the State Grand Lodge and the State Grand Encampment, the latter is subordinate to the State Grand Lodge.

2.—HOW THE LODGES ARE BOUND TOGETHER BY LAWS.

The Grand Lodge of the United States is the soul and main spring of the entire order; all the power and might rests in its hands. When it speaks, it is done; when it commands, every one must obey. It is provided by law, that, like as in the Order of Jesuits, everything acts upon the other, as the wheels in a machine; all parts are joined together, as links in a chain. Without its will, no one can, to use this expression, move hand or foot. It has its own Constitution and By-Laws,* and according to these every State Grand Lodge and Encampment must accommodate itself. No lodge can pass a resolution or law, which does not coincide in spirit with the same. The strictest and most punctual obedience is required of the State Grand Lodges, and these are admonished to hold all subordinate lodges to strict obedience in every respect (By-Laws of the G. L. U., Art. XX). No State Grand Lodge dare undertake to alter the "written" or the "unwritten" or "secret work," neither "sign" nor "grip," neither "pass-word" nor anything else. This power is vested only in the G. L. U. S. (See Constitution, Art. I). Every State Grand Lodge must hand in annually a correct report, wherein, for instance, the number of members, of those newly admitted, of the suspended, of the excommunicated, the receipts and the expenditures, &c., must be stated; so that at any hour it is able to tell the strength of the entire order. In short, the Grand Lodge of the United States has all the State Grand Lodges and Grand Encampments, with the great train of subordinate lodges and encampments, in tow, and leads them whither it pleases. It is the head of the great monster, and the tail follows willingly after.

---

* Both are to be found in the book: "Digest of the R. W. Grand Lodge of the United States I. O. O. F. 1871." To be had of G. Secretary James L. Ridgely, Baltimore, Md. Price, $2.50; with postage, $3.

Without questioning, the blinded troop follows through thick and thin, and in return has the pleasure to make weekly, monthly, quarterly, semi-annual, annual and casual payments, of which they and their families do not, on an average, receive the third part back. The "Grand Sire" reigns like a king, and, in his way, has a great deal more power than the President of the United States. According to the Constitution of the Grand Lodge of the United States, the State Grand Lodges can draw up their own constitution, which, of course, dare contain nothing which would smell of anything like opposition; neither has it validity until it has been approved and sanctioned by the G. L. U. S.

Almost the same relation exists between the subordinate lodges and the State Grand Lodges, as between the latter and the Grand Lodge of the United States, with this difference, that the subordinate lodges are still more gagged. These do not enjoy the right to draft their own constitution; the State Grand Lodge has drafted one for them, which they have simply to accept and to obey. It has only the right to make some by-laws suitable to its own circumstances, which must, of course, be in unison with the constitution, and are in many cases examined by the State Grand Lodge before they become valid. But every subordinate lodge has the privilege and the sacred duty to pay truly and honestly.

The entire form of government of the order is thoroughly despotic; indeed so much so, that the government of Russia seems liberal in comparison with it. The members of the subordinate lodges have, strictly taken, no real but only some apparent rights; yet, instead of them, a great many duties. They dare not send the representatives whom they like to the State Grand Lodge, but only such persons as the Grand Lodge has proposed to them, and those are the members of the lodge who have been Noble Grands. No member of a subordinate lodge can take part in the election of representatives to the Grand Lodge of the United States; they are much too low to do this; these are elected by the

State Grand Lodges and Encampments (Digest, p. 189). What would our American people say if members of Congress to be elected were in every case nominated by Congress in Washington, and the people could elect none other than these? Or if Congress should appoint a tribunal, which always elected the representatives of the people? Would this deserve the name of an election of the people? Would the people submit to such a thing? The Odd Fellows put up with all this, indeed sustain it with their money and by word.

Indeed, this order is a fearful power, a power of darkness. Here in the United States it numbers 400,000 adherents, all blindly obeying, and so soon as any one will not do so, he is expelled. Considering its pernicious doctrines, its shameful immorality, which, for example, approves of, protects and furthers perjury, it is inconceivable how a State can suffer such a community to exist in its midst, which, besides, holds all its sessions with closed doors. Least of all can it be understood how the Prussian government could grant such a society admission into its borders, and could revoke or elude the law of 1798, which forbids all secret societies standing in connection with foreign countries.* This may in a measure be explained by assuming that the respective gentlemen did not grant the Prussian government a complete and correct insight into their doctrine, form of government and morals, but, as always, only communicated so much as they found to serve their purposes. It is a melancholy fact, that Protestant governments for the last twenty years have more and more, directly or indirectly, favored societies with pernicious tendencies, as, for example, the order of Jesuits. We are the more astonished that Prussia favors this order, as history teaches how the mother of the Odd Fellows' order (order of Free Mason) repeatedly abused its power to the detriment of the State, as, for example, in France,

---

* See "Odd Fellow," July, 1871, p. 50 ff.

Spain and Germany.* That the daughter of Freemasonry will do the same as soon as circumstances are favorable and she finds it in her interest to do so, we need not doubt. On a small scale, the United States have already experienced this annually and every four years at the elections. Of what other use are the blinded members. They have vowed "to devote their lives to the brotherhood," to lend their brethren, "*in all circumstances of life,* . . . aid, counsel and protection," and the needy brother must not consider this "as a form merely, but *as a right*" (Pocket Comp., p. 13). The maxim of their founder, Wildey,† is impressed upon all the members of the order : "Save the country if possible, but at any rate save the order."‡

III.—SECRETS.

The order claims that its secrets are necessary for its existence. This is entirely correct; for, having assumed the obligation to aid and assist every brother first and foremost, in "all the circum-

---

* It might be interesting and timely to examine in how far secret societies have intrigued during our great civil war, and we would most pressingly recommend this subject to some one more able than we, for thorough examination.

† At all events, the toast given by Wildey, the founder of American Oddfellowship, at a supper given in New York (1859) on occasion of the fortieth anniversary of the existence of the order in America, which we find in "Heart and Hand" of Jan. 6th, 1872, is very characteristic of him; it is as follows : " May the enemies of Oddfellowship be rammed, damned and jammed into a seventy-four-pounder and blowed out of the touchhole." Notwithstanding such a horrible toast, which would not even become a New Zealand cannibal, the above paper asserts that Wildey during his whole life was ever endowed with the greatest reverence and esteem for religion. What kind of a religion might that be ?

‡ See Proceedings of the R. W. Grand Lodge of Wisconsin, 1858, p. 1228.

stances in life in which a brother may be placed," whether I am personally acquainted with him or not, I must, of course, possess a secret countersign whereby I can recognize him as an Odd Fellow. It is also necessary that I receive practical instruction in the manner of rendering aid, and that I exercise myself in the "grips," "signals of distress," &c., both in order to be continually ready to aid, as also to make myself known when I require aid and assistance. And, that the brethren do not perhaps aid a brother according to their own will and pleasure, but that he "in all circumstances of life" shall receive real aid, it is necessary that "*solemn promises*" *and oaths* should be taken in secret.

The secrets of the order can conveniently be divided into three classes.

1.—SIGNS OF RECOGNITION.

As signs of recognition, they use a number of pass-words; for example, the "evening word," "the Vice Grand's pass-word," "term pass-word." He alone who has the respective pass-word and can give the necessary "explanation" to it, is admitted into the lodge, and, that none other may enter, the outside "Sentinel with the sword" must watch. Concerning this Sentinel the Pocket Companion says (p. 165): "He should be a man of nerve, too,—one who would not for a moment hesitate to eject forcibly, if requisite, any person who might presume to deceive, or intrude upon, the lodge."

These "sacred" places are not for "listeners and thieves," "profane" and "unclean."

In order that brethren on a journey may not be incommoded, they have also a "traveling pass-word," "annual pass-word," &c.

"Grips" and "signs" belong also to the signs of recognition; all manner of signs with the hands and fingers, in order either to make one's self known to the brethren, to implore help, or to warn a brother; all manner of grips when shaking hands. All these signs of recognition are frequently changed, in order, if possible, to prevent the "profane" from becoming acquainted with them; should this once happen, it would cause a large expenditure of money, as new pass-words must be given out, which the order much prefers to deliver verbally by means of traveling officers.*

2.—THE CONFERRING OF DEGREES.

This is done in secret, and great care is taken that outsiders learn nothing about it. The lodges have five degrees, of which the second and fourth are of American invention, and the encampments have three; therefore eight in all. Besides these, there are officers' degrees, which, however, are considered as of secondary value.

Their books, containing the doctrines of the various degrees, the duties of the members and officers, and the introduction into the degrees and offices, are never sold to the "profane," so that the precious secrets may not come to the knowledge of the world. The books are called: "Charge Book, Degree Book, Instituting and Installation Book, Diagram, Encampment Ritual," &c. We cannot, therefore, make known the real secrets. However, the doctrines being of the most importance, and Rev. A. B. Grosh, author of the Manual, assuring us that they communicate the entire contents of their doctrines, yea, their every idea, to the world ("Odd Fellow" of April, 1871, p. 244), and referring us in the June number (p. 372), to his Manual, we will give these,

---

* The order has, however, a secret manner to communicate the respective pass-word by writing, when it seems impossible to do so by word of mouth. It is then written in cyphers, and, that the recipient may be able to decipher it, the "Key" is sent to him, which is a little book explaining the use of the cyphers for this purpose.

and examine whether they really have and contain something of worth, or whether they are sinful, ungodly, anti-christian and diabolical.

After a person has been initiated, has promised obedience, and vowed to devote his life to the brotherhood, without knowing what is expected of him (which no man can swear to as long as he has a Christian conscience left), after he has been frightened with all manner of hocus-pocus, and has seen the appropriate emblems of initiation, viz., a Skull and an Ax, he can receive the first, or *White Degree.*" On this occasion he learns "the importance of association for philanthropic purposes" (p. 153); that the laws of the lodge "extend the love of self-good to the love of mankind" (185); that when the members assist the "needy and suffering" of "the lodge," they themselves are made better. They therefore teach that the word of God is not true; for that teaches us that first the tree must become good, then it can also bring forth good fruit; the lodge, however, teaches, first do good works and thereby be made better. To introduce him into active brotherly love, that he never forsake a brother in distress, is the chief object of this degree, and he is told that when he is found walking therein, he is, like all "the charitable," an "imitator of God." But they do not refrain, even in conferring the first degree, from hinting, in some distant way, that he needs no Savior, by telling him that the "charitable" live "with a conscience void of offence toward God and man." If the poor man has now "evinced a willingness to enter into any proper obligation" (of course before he knows what it is), he will, sooner or later, in the second, or " *Covenant Degree,*" have an opportunity "of forming a still closer and more precious covenant with" his "brethren." With this "the covenanted friendship" is established, and the obligations of the same consist, according to page 171 ff, in this, that we " consider each other as friends, as brethren in soul, whom we would aid and support in affliction and persecution, whom we would rescue from impending peril, . . . the evil designs of enemies." He is taught "to guard the loved one from evil, to repel impending danger, and secure safety," and "that every laudable effort should be put forth to save a brother from the hand of an enemy" (p. 179). They endeavor, in this degree, to turn the eye of the "brother" away from the rest of mankind and to fix it alone upon the "brethren," to stand by them in all relations of life, to assist and to save them; whether right or wrong, these are very secondary considerations. To aid his brethren, that is the main point, and he has promised to do this. To encourage him in the fulfillment of this pledge, he is shown, among other things, the emblem of a Bundle of Rods, which cannot easily be broken together, and the Quiver and the Bow, with the admonition: "In peace prepare for war" (p. 177). But, as this cannot be done while a man believes in Christ and his word, whereby a Christian is put under obligation to serve all men, especially his *brethren in the faith*, also in this degree Christ as Redeemer, as he who must renew us by his spirit and give us strength to do good, must be set aside. Therefore the brother is instructed, in this degree, that he is now in a covenant, wherein *"each brother can easily resist evil and accomplish good"* (p. 177).

When the candidate has well understood the first two degrees, has come up to his obligations, of course with contempt of all Christianity, he can then receive the third, or "*Royal Blue Degree.*" On this occasion he hears the comforting instruction, that they desire of him not only to aid and to serve his brethren, but that he must also be ready to "sacrifice" himself for them, be they known or unknown to him, if they are only "members of the great family of Oddfellowship" (p. 181). As a true Odd Fellow, he must exercise "genuine friendship," and "meet sacrifice with firm resolve." He is also "specially instructed, in this degree," to "carefully and rigidly prove all who claim to be brethren." Confirmed in such resolutions by showing him the emblem of power, Moses' Rod, and that of cunning, the Serpent, he may for the present go on his way and prove his constancy. But they do not fail to point out to him the way of self-righteousness, as the brethren of this degree unanimously declare: "that if constant in our reverence of God, and in keeping his commandments," we "shall behold, amid all the storms and tempests of life, tokens of Divine approbation, and receive the visits of the celestial messenger, the Holy Spirit." They suppose, therefore, that they deserve the approbation of God, notwithstanding they reject his word entirely. True, they do deserve the approbation of *their God,* but not that of the living and true God.

"A brother who has studied well and practiced faithfully the principles of the preceding degrees, is prepared and worthy to enter into the obligations of the "*Degree of Remembrance,*" which is the fourth degree. This degree is intended to help him over the boundaries of "confessions of faith," "communities" and "sects." He shall, as a genuine Odd Fellow, arrive at the conviction that he is far exalted above every Christian confession of faith; that he stands high above such barriers, and that the word of God therefore has no right, furthermore, to set him such boundaries. And, as these principles are so powerful to banish "discordant feelings" and "prejudices" from earth and to "make the world a Paradise," they give him a gentle hint, in this degree, that he must seek to spread them; declare, among other things, on page 196, that the love of man is even prerequisite to the love of God, and "mankind is our family, our country the earth, our nation the human race." To awaken in him love for the "work," he is shown the emblem of the Horn of Plenty, which will now most assuredly pour out upon him the entire fullness of riches, of joy and of prosperity, and the emblem of constraining justice, the Sword, in order to be ready "to defend the right, even (if need be) unto death" (p. 206). And so he comes into possession of the "many beauties and merits" of this degree.

When the fourfold degraded man has made good progress in the "duties and labors" of the lodge, he can finally receive the fifth, or "*Scarlet Degree.*"* This is dedicated to truth, but by no means to the truth of sacred writ, but to the truth of his own heart's shrine. Everything that his own heart "dictates," in religious matters, is right and true; and this truth shall direct him how to act. This is "the Degree of the Priestly Order." Every brother of this degree is to "represent" Aaron, as "priest and monarch of himself and all around him"; "as such, he is an example in speech and action, *blessing and purifying others.*" The lodge expects of every one who has received this degree, that he "understand and preserve inviolate" its "mysteries, and to observe that his brethren do the same"; the more so, because now "all stations of the lodge" are open to him, and he can enter as one who "is enabled to speak as by authority." Therefore he is also charged: "Correct the errors and confirm the faith of your brethren; it is your office, your *right*, your *duty*." He must "strive to hasten the period when *every man* shall be . . . a priest," and shall assure the brethren "that God is our Father, and will make us the sharers of His immortality and *eternal life*" (Compare p. 210–222).

After the poor man has now been caught in the net of the lodge, and by degrees has learned to love its doctrine, that the old Adam loves so well, and has received the five degrees and paid for them his hard-earned money (for every degree costs its "sum," usually two dollars), he will "naturally desire to advance further" (p. 355), in order to receive the three "sublime" degrees of the encampment, "with their rich stores of instruction." "Every Odd Fellow should make it his aim to reach the topmost round of the ladder of Oddfellowship, the

---

* When a dispensation is granted by the Grand Master, all the five degrees can be conferred at once.

Royal Purple Degree" (Pocket Comp., p. 197), so that the encampment may also receive from him the handsome sums of entrance fee and the monthly, yearly and other contributions, and can give him further light. If the poor and egregiously deluded man resolves to take this degree, he must apply for it in writing, enclosing the initiation fee (twelve to twenty dollars), and can then, if chosen by ballot, receive the first encampment degree, *the Patriarchal*. On this occasion he is instructed, that virtue is above all things; and that it is his duty particularly to exercise hospitality to the brother patriarchs, and that these "especially" must receive his "sympathy" and "aid." Those who obligate themselves to do so are admonished: "If ye *know* these things, happy are ye if ye *do* them." To strengthen him in his purpose, three pillars are shown him, with the explanation that these are the Wisdom, Strength and Beauty of Religion, and the supports and ornaments of our Temple of Universal Brotherhood" (Compare Manual, p. 365-373). If the "patriarch" now practices all the virtues, well enough; but this does not suffice. He lacks yet the greatest light and the deepest mystery; this shall now be imparted and revealed to him in the "*Golden Rule Degree.*" And what is now the greatest light of the order, that the candidate, at his initiation into this degree, receives? It shines forth from the following declarations: "Confessions of faith" are "differences of opinion." "In our Tents no sectarian or national distinctions are recognized." "*Followers of different Teachers, —ye are worshipers of One God*, who is Father of all, and *therefore ye are brethren*"! "The descendants of Abraham, the diverse followers of Jesus, the Patriarchs of the stricter sects (these are Heathen in the East Indies. The Author.), here gather around the same altar, as one family, *manifesting no differences of creed or worship.*" "They have left their prejudices at the door, and mingle in one circle of brotherhood, harmony and love" (Man., pp. 874-388). "It heeds not whether the man be a . . . Jew or Heathen"

(Pocket Comp., p. 306). "Jew or Gentile, Catholic or Protestant, is, *as such*, welcome to our lodges and our hearts" (Pocket Comp., p. 307). We unite with every man "in practising those great precepts which belong to all religions" (Manual, p. 384). "*The authority of conscience, in religion, must be paramount*" (Manual, p. 376). And, as these principles are so infinitely weighty and necessary for the improvement of the human race, "let us, then, not cease its practice, while we urge the reasons for our faith. On it let us all unite in furthering the mission of Oddfellowship" (Manual, p. 384). We will therefore seriously endeavor to convert to our faith all "who bow not at our altar." (p. 386).

With these declarations the order has proclaimed its mongrel religion, that is, a heathen religion, which every Jew, Gentile, Chinese, African and Hottentot has by nature. Christ, with his work of redemption, is made perfectly superfluous; instead of the word of God, the perverted conscience, estranged from God, is set up as the rule and standard of religion. If, perhaps, until then, the lodge member has yet been loosely connected with Christianity, this connection ceases entirely so soon as he has received this degree and believes this doctrine. Heathenish doctrine is restored, in its plainest and most marked form; Christ is denied, and placed on the same footing with Confucius, Budda and Zoroaster,* and man, estranged from Christ and his word, pointed to his own corrupt heart and conscience, in matters of religion.

---

* This is literally done in the "Odd Fellow" of August, 1871, p. 114, where it is said: "Who were the most renowned teachers of religion and morals of the olden time? Who were the men who first gave these ideas a definite form and delivered them as systematic moral principles to their fellow-men and pressed them upon their acceptance, just as they are to-day LAID DOWN IN ODDFELLOWSHIP ? We know five,—Moses, Budda, Confucius, Zoroaster and Christ." The order, however, cannot accomplish much with Moses; he can consequently be "left out of consideration," as he is too strict in his laws.

And to *this faith* the order will convert all; that is its mission. May God have mercy!

There is one more, the last degree,—the "*Royal Purple Degree*," which is the symbol of rest, and in it they, according to their own assurances, enjoy a foretaste "of the immortal glorious repose of immortality itself." The candidate is received into it with music, and instructed that, as he has now received the "full light" of the "order," he must also let his light shine and follow its principles. Then let death come; he need not fear it, because these principles "alone can convert his conquest into our triumph, even make us *more* than conquerors over the last enemy" (Manual, p. 397). He can repose his head on the pillow of "content" and come up "to the land of eternal delight."

To the secrets of the order must be reckoned also the installation and swearing in of the officers. What duties are imposed upon them more than is publicly made known, is not communicated to the "profane." It is sufficient that we know that they all are contradictory to the word of God.

Sometimes these gentlemen would fain count their benefactions, inside and outside of the order, among their secrets; but we cannot suffer them to do so, as the so-called benefactions within the order are annually published in many reports. And what is here and there done outside of the order, they generally take good care to make known to the world in some form or other. A society of Odd Fellow ladies in Washington, D. C., spent, for example, in 1870, $1500 for benevolent purposes, but much pains is taken that this is published to the world through the press, as, for instance, in the "Odd Fellow" of June, 1861, page 373. In the Eastern States, a number of lodges (perhaps some two dozen) some time ago collected money scarcely sufficient to send the widow of an Odd Fellow, with some children, to Germany, and a number of papers extolled them in the most extravagant terms. Those who do not recognize the word of God in general, will pay no regard to the words in Matt. 6 : 1–3, much less will they act up to them.

Since 1851, the order has seen fit to admit "ladies" into the lodge, and to establish the "Rebecca Degree." The wives of Odd Fellows, who have taken the five degrees, can be admitted, and are then called "The daughters or Sisters of Rebecca." The establishment of this "degree" is certainly of advantage to the order, as the unbelieving women of our land, in politics, antichristian agitations and the practice of abortions, form a power by no means to be despised. Besides, the lodge brothers would miss an immense intellectual advantage, if their better halves did not belong to the lodge; for they sing : "The purest light will shine around us, when woman's goodness beams on us" ("Odd Fellow" of Nov., 1870, p. 697; Feb., 1871, p. 116). What a terribly impure and foul light must accordingly "shine around" them when "woman's perfection" does not beam on them! They have, however, found it advisable, up to this present time, to leave the women in the ante-chamber, and to communicate to them only a very small part of the precious secrets, as they only receive one degree, while men, beside the officers' degrees, can attain to eight degrees. Indeed, up to this date, they are not even allowed to elect from among them a Mistress of the Chair. Those who claim for women the ballot are therefore still far from having attained the "equality of all races." The whole farce is, until now, only a mockery of women's right to vote.

3.—OATHS.

All the obligations of the order are taken under oath, or promises that have the force of an oath. Every member must, at his initiation, promise, by oath : to obey the lodge and its laws, to devote his life to the brotherhood, and to observe the strictest silence in respect to the "secret work" of the order.

As we have already shown, all the officers must swear also, in assuming their obligations. To be sure, the Manual (p. 74) falsely declares: "We are not, therefore, an oath-bound institution, nor are our obligations *oaths*.' But, that their obligations really are oaths, the Manual itself admits (p. 410): "The receiver of this degree [the Grand Encampment Degree] *appeals to heaven and earth* to witness the fidelity with which he will represent the interests of his subordinates, and at the same time faithfully preserve the secrets, advance the interests, and promote the welfare of his Grand Encampment." That to "appeal unto Heaven and Earth" is swearing, we learn from Matthew 5 : 34, 35. Therefore the assumed obligations are never considered and treated otherwise than as taken on oath. In the "Odd Fellow" of July, 1870, p. 534, it is said of the members of secret societies: "By the *oath* which unites them .... a power over the individual is exercised, which no one can understand, who has not personally felt its influence." From page 697, of November, 1870, and page 54, of January, 1871, we learn that at the initiation of the Sisters of Rebecca, they are charged, in song: "*Swear* by active silence,—*swear* in the fullness of the spirit." But, what oaths are sworn in the dead of the night, behind the "Sentinels with the Sword," we cannot even guess at, as no more of them is published than what the lodge thinks fit.*

---

* As regards the oaths, it is a matter of fact, that the Order of Odd Fellows have done away with and moderated the dreadful and repulsive forms which were until lately in use in the Order of Free Masons. But the oath they have retained, even if it is not always sworn by the "living God." In the Free Masons' oath the following passage occurs: "I vow and swear hereby, in the presence of Almighty God, that I will never reveal the secrets .... All this under no less punishment, than that my throat shall be cut, my tongue rent from the root of my mouth, my heart torn out from under my left breast, . . . my body burned to ashes, and my ashes scattered over the surface of the earth." See Constitution of the Free Masons, of 1723, and Hengstenberg's "Freemasonry and the Evangelical Ministry," p. 47 ff.

We must further count among the secrets, the obligation to silence toward members of the lodge themselves, or the secrets of the members among each other. No one who, for example, has taken the fifth degree, dare divulge to his "brother" of the fourth degree the secrets of the fifth degree; neither dare one who has received the fourth degree, communicate its "secret" to his brethren of the third degree. No brother of a higher grade dare reveal its secrets to those who have not yet received the respective degrees; and so the pitiable mysteriousness pervades the whole order.† The brotherly love of the members of the lodge does not permit them to communicate the "sublime doctrines" of the higher degree to the brethren of the subordinate degrees, that they might be "made better men." No; it is shackled completely by their trash of secrecies. And, should a "brother" be too poor to pay for the higher degrees, he cannot receive the "full light of the order," but must eternally languish in the twilight.

But, for what reason must the order have "secrets"? A number of answers to this question have, directly or indirectly, been given; but we will only state one given in the Odd Fellow of April, 1871, page 244, which reads as follows: because "they draw new members into our lodges"! The world loves to be fooled, and the lodges know this.

---

* Secrets pervade the whole order. It is impossible that one brother can trust the other, not knowing what secrets he has. During the assembly of the Grand Lodge of the United States, which holds all its sessions in secret, they hold extra secret sessions, to which the Grand Sire admits only some elect. These sessions are therefore, with the exception of the few elect persons, secret to the whole order, even to those who have received every possible "degree." See "Heart and Hand," No. 96, 1872. In these doubly secret sessions the plans are devised, for the execution of which, so many members, unknown to themselves, suffer themselves to be made use of.

IV.—ACTIVITY.

"The first business of a lodge is, of course, to increase its membership" (Pocket Comp., p. 151). "Wedging" is one of the duties of the lodge members. The subordinate lodges are called "working lodges," chiefly because they have to draw others into the lodge by the mighty power of persuasion; and this most of the members do. They exert themselves in and outside of the beer saloon, to persuade men and induce them to join their lodge. That in this "work" Truth is an entirely subordinate consideration; that they work cunningly, like serpents, is a matter of course. If they have to deal with one who is religiously inclined, they seek to convince him, by all manner of lies, that the lodge esteems Christianity very highly; that on that account it makes use of the Bible, prays and sings; that it is the lodge that really obeys the command of God, to do good to the widows and orphans, and that the secret societies have been "the conservators .... of religious ... truth" (Manual, p. 17). If they have an unbeliever before them, he is pointed to the great advantages offered by the lodge; he is told that the dues are very small, but the aid received is very material. And in such a case they succeed more easily if the person addressed has a large family and no certain means of support; but these are not the most sought after.*

Is this every subordinate lodge's "first business," "to increase its membership," so it is the task of the more influential members to win others of influence and respectability to the order. Toward

---

* We must also reckon among the means of drawing persons into the lodge, the visits to the sick, which are chiefly made for this purpose, as is plainly seen from their writings. See, for example, "Lodge Bulletin" of October, 1871.

such the high morality and glorious liberality of the order is extolled, and how much good they can accomplish through their influence, if they should unite with it. Great joy prevails everywhere, if they succeed in winning a prominent person. With no small degree of self-esteem, the order boasts that very many Congressmen in Washington are members of their order; that even the ex-Vice-President, Schuyler Colfax, is a "brother." Such "brothers" in high standing must use all the influence of their position to promote the welfare of the order. And that "brothers" be elected to Congress and to every possible office, every one in the lodge, great and small, looks to. Many people who do not belong to the lodge, neither are acquainted with the workings of these "brethren," place them in office by their votes; of course, ignorantly. Did all Christians know the nature and principles of the order, certainly no one would vote for one of its members. Nor is it possible, that a member of a lodge, who has promised, by oath, firstly and above all other things, "to seek the welfare of the order and the brethren," can impartially seek and promote the welfare of the entire country and all classes of our population. If, for example, he be chosen as representative, he must either break his oath to the lodge (and that scarcely one out of a thousand will do) and impartially strive for the good of all classes of the population, or he must first "seek the good of the order," whereby, as a matter of course, the others are more or less at a disadvantage.

It would probably have been very difficult for the order to gain entrance into Prussia, had not our former Vice-President, Mr. Colfax, brought to bear the whole weight of his position in favor of the order. In consequence of this influence, and, very likely, also in consequence of jesuitical art of persuasion, Baron v. Gerolt, North German Ambassador in Washington, was favorably inclined to the doctrines and practices of the Odd Fellows, and also "transmitted to his government a highly favorable report of of the Order" * ("Odd Fellow" of July, 1871, p. 51; Proceedings of the G. L. U. S., 1871, p. 5515 ff.).

In seeking, with special preference, to win influential persons to the order, they do not, however, neglect to draw the attention of all classes upon themselves. This is accomplished by means of pompous processions, public installations of the officers of the lodge, and through the press. The public installation of their officers is an invention of modern times. Their object is clearly expressed in "Heart and Hand" of October 5th, 1870, where it says: "They (the public installations) draw attention to the order. A lodge may exist in a place for years, and is known only to its members. A public ceremony has the effect of bringing our fellow-citizens into our halls." For this reason, they take great pains to make them very ostentatious. The world likes to be fooled.

---

* In order to introduce Oddfellowship into Germany, after the Grand Lodge of the United States had passed the respective resolution at its session in California, 1869, Dr. J. L. Morse was nominated as Special Deputy for Germany and Switzerland, and commissioned to do everything in his power to introduce the order into those countries. According to his own report, which he handed in to the G. L. U. S. in Chicago in 1871, he founded on the 1st of December, 1870, Wurtemburg Lodge No. 1, in Stuttgart; on the 2d of April, 1871, Germania Lodge No. 1, in Berlin; on the 23d of May, Farnsworth Encampment, in the same place; on the 6th of June, Saxonia Lodge No. 1, in Dresden; and on the 10th of June, Helvetia Lodge No. 1, in Berne. He had scarcely left Germany when, already in July, the second lodge, Borussia Lodge No. 2, was established in Berlin. (See Proceedings Grand Lodge of the United States, p. 5007 ff.) On the 9th of December, 1871, a lodge was founded in Berlin which "works" in the English language, for the convenience of the American Odd Fellows traveling in Germany. According to the latest report of the G. L. U. S. (of 1873), there are now in existence in Germany and Switzerland 19 lodges and 16 encampments. Since the 1st of October, 1871, a paper appears in Berlin, edited by Wilh. Altvater and Paul Juhre, under title "Heart and Hand," which is in the interest of the order. (See "Heart and Hand," Jan. 6th, 1872.)

The lodge is well acquainted with the influence of the press, and therefore exerts itself to make industrious use of it for its own purposes. The order itself has a number of periodicals, about a dozen, in which they praise up to the world their good works, their high morality and toleration. These papers are partly official, partly edited and published by prominent members of the order, and they still endeavor to increase their number. They also take pains to win the entire press of the country, as far as possible, to their side, and, wherever it is practicable, to bring an Odd Fellow into the editor's chair; and if they do not succeed in this, at least to send, from time to time, to the most popular papers, articles for publication, filled with glorifications of the order.

The order has a regular system of aid for cases of sickness and death. Every one in "good standing," who is not indebted to the lodge, or does not stand under any charge, receives, in case of sickness, weekly, the appointed sum (usually from three to fifteen dollars). If his wife dies, he receives the funeral expenses (from fifteen to twenty-five dollars). If a brother dies, his wife receives double this sum. The widows and orphans of the brothers are not provided for according to any established rule. If an Odd Fellow's widow applies to the lodge for support, and the committee of investigation find her needy, they generally grant her aid. They act in a similar manner toward the orphans, for whom they have already founded a number of orphan asylums, with schools, and are intending to establish still more.*

Lately, almost all the State Grand Lodges have instituted Life-Insurance Leagues for their members, in such a manner that at the death of a brother, every member of this Life-Insurance League

---

* The order has also occupied itself, for the past few years, with the erection of colleges, in order to obtain scientifically educated members, from whom they naturally expect very advantageous results to the lodges. Everything like with the Jesuits.

must pay a fixed sum (usually one dollar), and the wife of the deceased receives as many dollars as there are members in the society; the number of members does not usually exceed 2000 to 3000.

In the large cities, where there are several lodges, they have begun to read a list of all the brothers that are without employment, in every meeting of the lodge, so that all who have or know of employment, can be of aid to them in procuring it. Besides all this, the order considers every member morally bound, where it is at all possible, to employ brothers, in case he must employ some one. The Grand Encampment of Wisconsin resolved, for instance, in the year 1871, to allow no one but a member of the order to print the Report of their Convention, their Constitution and By-Laws.*

But all these are secondary matters, only "means to the end," "hardly a tithe of their aims and objects." The chief aim is and will be, to "reform the world," and to "convert all men to their faith." But members do not learn this before they are themselves converted (or rather perverted) to the faith of the order. When that has taken place, it is enjoined upon them, in the "Golden Rule Degree," as their duty.

According to the Proceedings of the Grand Lodge of the United States, of 1873, p. 5671, the order had 385,097 members, in 5045 lodges, and we apprehend that by far the greater portion of the members are already converted to *its* faith. The report of the Convention of the G. L. U. S., of September, 1873, states an increase of 57,220 members and 753 lodges, according to page 5800. Weeds grow apace. This is certainly an earnest admonition to every Christian: Wake up, thou that sleepest!

---

* See Proceedings of the Grand Encampment. 1871, p. 232.

V.—WHETHER IT IS PROFITABLE TO JOIN THE LODGE.

We will not enter here into the unmeasurable detriment to the soul which the acceptance of the lodge's doctrine entails, and which must be its consequence; for this cannot be calculated, neither according to degree nor time. Loss of faith in Christ carries with it everlasting condemnation. We will only briefly inquire, how great the material advantage or damage is, which one has in consequence of joining the lodge. This can be calculated and stated in dollars and cents. We deem this the more necessary, as, alas! it is by promises of earthly advantages that, as we believe, most members have been and are daily gained for the order.

"*Christian*," in his conversation with "*Ernest*," proves from several Reports, that not quite the third part of the money paid into the lodge is expended for purposes of relief; yet this proportion, on the whole, is not generally even reached. "Heart and Hand," a paper "for Odd Fellows and Daughters of Rebecca," of September 2d, 1871, teaches us better. It says: "We notice in an exchange the startling query that the Odd Fellows have a revenue of four millions annually, and that they expend in relief *only one million* dollars a year, and 'what becomes of the other three millions?' If a man makes a hundred thousand dollars a year, and gives away one or two thousand to worthy objects, he is reckoned a liberal-minded, charitable gentleman. And so he is. But the Odd Fellows give away one-fourth of their gross receipts, and, ignoring this fact entirely, some dissatisfied, jealous growler says, with as much eagerness as if he contributed the whole of it, 'Where is the rest of the money?' Well, we will tell. In the first place, one-fourth of it goes for the relief of brethren and widows, burying the dead, and educating the orphan. In the second place, Odd Fellows have to pay for rent, fuel, and service done at their meetings, just the same as if they were other human beings. Their furniture, regalia, and appointments, not being of indestructible material, strange as it may appear, frequently need replacing, and people charge them for the same, as though they were ordinary mortals. To run an establishment of 4000 lodges requires rooms, halls, &c., and we generally have good ones. Every one of our 325,000 members and 68,000 officers must have regalia appropriate," &c., &c. Therefore the Odd Fellow Lodges expend only, according to their own admission, the fourth part of their income for purposes of relief; almost three-fourths of their income is swallowed up by officers, regalia, lodge-rooms, furniture, traveling expenses of the officers, &c. And yet they boast a great deal of their charities, and imagine that if they expended only $2000 out of every $100,000 for purposes of relief, they should justly be accounted "liberal-minded and charitable," like the man they cite. From this it is evident, that when a lodge member has paid in $100, he receives, on an average, $25 back. On paying $400, he may, as a general thing, expect $100. No common mutual-aid society has, to this day, done as badly as this. Then must be counted in the many extra expenses of the members, as for "wedging," for their regalia, with their ornaments, and so forth, often amounting to a considerable sum annually.

Whoever, therefore, wishes to get rid of his money, and to inflict temporal and eternal damage upon his soul, let him unite with the lodge! To be sure the afore mentioned paper says that the order (that is, all the subordinate lodges, all the State Grand Lodges and the Grand Lodge of the United States, taken together) owns property to the value of twenty million dollars. How much of this sum the poor will receive, time must determine. Our expectations are not very great. Judging by what has hitherto been done by the lodge, they do not even receive the hundredth part.

But, should it really not be profitable to join the lodge, as by doing so one receives more aid, can more easily find employment, and if one is a mechanic or merchant, gains many customers? Every one may find the answer to this question from experience. If you pay attention, you will observe that, regularly, out of every ten bankrupts, eight belong to the Free Masons or Odd Fellows. If the promised mutual aid brought the hoped-for earthly advantages, this rule would have to be reversed, so that of every ten bankrupts two, at the uttermost, were Odd Fellows or Free Masons. But we do not find this to be the case. Or is the supposition perhaps correct, that they declare themselves bankrupt in order to make money thereby? This would indeed be a fatal witness against the highly extolled morality of the order.

That the lodge does not afford aid from motives of and according to charity, but only where there is a legal obligation to do so, is the natural consequence of its doctrines; and experience, as well as the official reports of the order, confirms this fact. From the great multitude of examples of this kind we will only furnish a few, and these such as have been officially published by the order itself. We take these from "Minutes of the Grand Lodge of I. O. O. F. of Pennsylvania, 1871." On page 492 ff. it is reported that Henry L. Genther, member of the "Old Monongahela Lodge No. 209, in Elizabeth, Alleghany Co., Pa.," who claimed the constitutional funeral expenses, as his wife had died. On the 29th of November, 1870, he made his application to the lodge, but the Noble Grand decided that he was not entitled to relief. Genther appealed, and represented in writing that he mailed a registered letter containing five dollars, addressed to the Secretary of the lodge, on the 4th day of October, 1870, at Braidwood, Illinois, and claimed that the money, from the time he mailed that registered letter, ceased to be his property and became the property of the lodge (according to our opinion, quite correctly), and on the 8th of October (therefore four days later) his wife died;

that he was therefore, at the time of her death, not indebted to the lodge; on the contrary, had a balance in his favor, and was on that account entitled to relief. But the lodge declared that the money was not received and credited until the 11th of October, and up to that time he owed the lodge $3.59, and that amount was placed to his credit under that date, and the remainder of $1.41 entered in his favor. However, the money not arriving until three days after the death of his wife, he was not entitled to receive the funeral expenses. Genther replied, that as he lived some 100 miles distant from his lodge, he could not possibly be made responsible for the time when the money should arrive, if he mailed it in good time in a registered letter. But it was all of no avail; the decision of the Noble Grand was sustained. This affair was then brought up before a Board of Appeal of the State Grand Lodge of Pennsylvania; but its decision was the same; so that the lodge might keep its money. Whoever owes the lodge but five cents, gets nothing, no matter whether he has paid for one year or thirty years, if the money does not come at the right time. no matter whether through his fault or without his fault.

How much the lodge cares for the widows and orphans, another example may illustrate. On page 486 ff. of the above mentioned document, we find the following story: Jacob Daumb, member of the Chambersburg Lodge No. 175, Chambersburg, Franklin Co., Pa., removed some nine years ago to Fort Wayne, Indiana Co., Pa., and remitted his dues from there to the lodge. He sent the last five dollars in the month of February, 1869, and it was placed to his credit the 5th of March of the same year. This sum not only covered his indebtedness, but left a balance of seventy-five cents in his favor. The by-laws of his lodge provide that no member is entitled to any benefits until four weeks after he has paid his indebtedness. On the 29th of March J. Daumb suddenly died, and the question arose, "Is the widow, Elizabeth Daumb, entitled to the funeral expenses?" The lodge decided, "No," because on the 5th of March the five dollars were placed to his credit, and on the 29th of the same month he died, therefore before the four weeks had expired ; for this reason she is not entitled to relief. This matter was also laid before the Board of Appeal of the State Grand Lodge, but that gave the same decision ; so that the lodge might retain the money ; and the widow, whether needy or not, received nothing. From this it is very apparent that the lodge cunningly seeks to withhold its benefits, wherever it can find a plausible pretext to do so, even when it is morally, yea legally bound to render them, as in this case. The man had paid "some time in the month of February," as the lodge itself declares. February had, in the year 1869, only 28 days. As he had paid in the month of February, it could not have been later than on the 28th, this being the last day of the month ; from the 28th of February till the 29th of March, the day of his death, it is, as everybody knows, over four weeks, and accordingly his widow was entitled to receive the funeral expenses, according to the by-laws of that lodge. But the Secretary had not entered the sum till the 5th of March, and the lodge chose to reckon from that date, because it was to its own interest ; and so they left the widow without aid. As in the first case, the man was made responsible for the management and delivery of the mail, so in this case the widow is made responsible for the Secretary's faithful discharge of his duties. It is easy to understand that in this and similar ways the lodge can "make money" with ease. There is no appeal from the decision of the Grand Lodge.

This is the way the lodge acts toward "brothers" and "sisters." What, then, can those expect who are not members, or who are opposed to secret societies? The much vaunted "love" and "brotherhood" extends, at best, just as far as the payments reach, but not a hair breadth further. Indeed its motto, "love," is, in the fullest sense of the word, an immense lie.

VI. — HOW THE ORDER AGREES WITH THE PRINCIPLES OF OTHER SECRET SOCIETIES, ESPECIALLY WITH THE DOCTRINES OF THE FREE MASONS.*

All the secret societies, of which there are a great many in this country (according to the "Odd Fellow," almost a hundred), agree in their fundamental principles (at least we have not yet found a single exception). All have the same religious principles, the same doctrine, the same religion, namely natural religion, pretending to recognize a Supreme Being, whom every one can and shall serve according to the desires of his heart and the selfish voice of his conscience, for which they of course cannot and will not use the word of God, and making its mission to reform the world and to "convert" it "to their belief." Besides the Odd Fellows and Free Masons, out of the great number of secret societies, we mention only a few, as: Druids, Harugari, Red Men, Knights of Pythias, Sons of Herman, No Surrenders, Good Fellows, the Order of the Seven Wise Men, Sons of Temperance, Good Templars, the Order of B'nai B'rith, the Order of St. Crispin, &c., &c., to which must be added the Order of the "Foresters," which was established here about 1863; its first "District Court" was founded in New York in 1864, and it carries its devastations

---

* According to the Report of the Grand Lodge of Free and Accepted Masons of the United States, of 1871, this order numbers, in the United States and Canada, 454,355 members. Whoever wishes to gain a more particular insight into the nature and practice of this anti-christian order, to him we recommend the work, "Acacia Blossoms from the Free Masons' Order," by F. W. A. Riedel, Evang. Pastor; a book manifesting diligent study and Christian sentiment.

not only among adults but also among the young; and the **Patrons** of Husbandry, established about 1867.

Not one of these orders rests upon the foundation of the divine word; they all confess the universal religion of the natural man. Every member of such an order makes unto himself a God according to his own pleasure and the imaginations of his evil heart, just as he likes to have him, and then he represents him to be the "Creator and Preserver of the Universe." Should this purely imaginary deity after a while cease to please him, or has it gone out of fashion, he can be remodeled as occasion requires, or indeed an entirely new one manufactured. Every one having his own God, each one will of course endeavor to convert others to his God, and this is the way in which unity shall be restored to the distracted world. We are most anxious to see this unity and this "glorious epoch." The Lord our God once said to his people: "According to the number of thy cities were thy gods" (Jer. 11:13). As regards the lodge, this would be saying too little. It would suit it better to say: "According to the number of thy members are thy gods." Indeed we would like to see two members of the order who have, honor and worship one and the same God.

Just as the different secret societies coincide in the principles of natural or heathen religion, so in their form of government they all rest upon one and the same basis, namely, that of the law, or, more correctly speaking, of despotism. And this at least partly explains the very close relation in the form of government and administration. In every order the members are linked together by rules; the iron straight jacket is laid on every one, and he is robbed of a great part of his personal freedom. In all the orders the oath, here in a more shocking and there in a milder form, plays an important roll and is a strong tie.

It would of course transcend the narrow limits of this little book, should we endeavor to prove the agreement in **doctrines and** principles of about a dozen of these Orders, as shown in their books of instruction, constitutions, papers, &c.* We content ourselves, therefore, with giving, as concisely as possible, an abstract of the principal doctrines of the Free Masons, in order to furnish the proof that the doctrines of the Odd Fellows and Free Masons are as much alike as one egg is like the other, or one hand resembles the other. We take this short statement of doctrine from Macoy: "The Free Masons' Manual. A Pocket Companion for the Initiated. Translated into the German by J. P. Finkelmeier. New York, 1870." On page 5 is said: Freemasonry is an order founded by virtuous men for the noble design of preserving in us, watchful and active, the sense for the most sublime truths in the midst of innocent and social pleasures. Founded upon noble-mindedness, brotherly love and benevolence, it is a glorious system of morality." This order has the Bible, chaplains, sermons, prayers, and allmanner of religious ceremonies. It believes, like the Odd Fellows, in a "Supreme Being." The order publishes to the world that the foundation upon which Free Masonry rests is "faith in and acknowledgment of a Supreme Being" (p. 12). But we should be very much mistaken should we imagine that they rest alone upon that basis. This foundation alone is entirely too weak. In order to prevent the danger of breaking through this weak foundation, they add another to it. And what is it? Geometry! Concerning this we read on page 62: "Geometry, the noblest of sciences, *is the foundation upon which the edifice of Freemasonry is erected.*" And on page 4 the candidate is "particularly recommended" to "study geometry, which forms the foundation of our art." The order says (p. 21): "The entire

---

* Whoever wishes further information concerning the doctrines and principles of the different secret societies, we recommend to him "The Christian Cynosure," edited by E. A. Cook, 13 Wabash Ave., Chicago, Ill.; weekly edition $2.

universe is the temple of the *Divinity which we adore.*" And this self-invented divinity is so terribly bold as to enact "laws," and to demand that we "should render it that reasonable homage" which the Free Masons declare "constitutes the summary of our duties and our felicity" (p. 43). Freemasonry teaches "the duties we owe to God, our neighbors and ourselves" (p. 66). And what is the source of this instruction? We hear, on page 67: "The brothers of this degree (the third), who have maintained unimpaired the ancient landmarks of our order, *are the source from which we derive that treasure of instruction and information.*" They have, then, of course, no need of the sacred Scriptures as "source" of the knowledge of salvation. The Free Masons declare, solemnly and in all seriousness, on page 34: "No institution was ever established on better principles or erected on a firmer foundation." The Christian Church, which is founded upon the word of Almighty God, and upon the blood of our everlasting High Priest, has, according to this, a much weaker "foundation" and much worse "principles." The Free Masons even believe in "that heavenly lodge, where the Supreme Architect of the Universe presides" (p. 18). To get there is naturally their desire; but how to accomplish it? Well, that is very simple. This place is "the starry heaven which all good Masons hope finally to reach, by the *aid of that spiritual ladder,* which Jacob saw in his dream extending from earth to heaven" (p. 22). "Every one must *merit* the evidence of a contented conscience" (p. 108); must render punctual obedience to the laws and ordinances of the lodge; then they can, "as Master Masons, enjoy in old age the blissful fruits of a well-spent life, and *depart from hence in the confidence of a glorious immortality*" (p. 75). On their death bed "the happy remembrance of a virtuously spent life will be their sole consolation" (p. 124). We must, however, in accordance with the everlasting word of God, exclaim: Woe, woe unto him who has no other consolation upon his dying bed!

And, finally, these mistaken souls imagine their self-invented deity, the Grand Master of that heavenly lodge, will call to them from the starry heaven: "Come, ye blessed of my Father. inherit the kingdom prepared for you from the foundation of the world" (p. 128).

But in the meanwhile they are still upon earth, and there are many "duties" for them to fulfill. Above all things, obedience and observation of the constitution is required. If any one is uncertain about anything, he is referred to the "Book of the Constitution," the law and gospel of Freemasonry. We read concerning the Constitution, on page 23: "As certain guides to an exemplary life, unerring rules, with which every lodge is provided, are suggested to the Free Mason. The law book lies before him, that he cannot say, he erred through ignorance; and what the grand Architect of the Universe has ever ordained, as the way to glorify him; the path of virtue in which he desires us to walk the directions which he has ever given to attain his approbation, as well as the laws which he announced through the wise men of antiquity,—are all faithfully laid down in the law book of Freemasonry. This book reveals the duties which the Grand Master has imposed upon us, clearly and openly, and intelligible to every intellect; who among us durst, then, say he was ignorant of the true worship." The "grand Architect of the world" has given and promulgated laws through the "wise men of antiquity." Who were these "wise men"? They were the wise men of the heathen Greeks and Romans, who worshiped idols. The "great Architect of the Universe" is therefore in perfect unity of the faith with these Heathen. This agreement of doctrine we really find in the constitution, that is, coincidence in doctrine with all Free Masons, with whom the "great Architect of the Universe" is in perfect harmony, as he is said to have given these ordinances and laws. Their constitution says, among other things, that they find it expedient to bind their members "*alone to that religion in* *which all mankind agree.*" * What is, then, this religion in which all men by nature agree? That there is one God only? No. That there is a Triune God? Oh, no. That Jesus is the Son of God? By no means! That he has redeemed us by his blood? Not at all! That there is a hell for the impenitent and unbelievers? On no account! What is it, then? Do right, fear no one; if there is a heaven, you will surely go there. In this religion, it is true, all men by nature agree, as well as in the article: Believe what you please, nothing depends upon faith.

Every journyman Free Mason is admonished: "You are bound zealously to support our laws and ordinances" (p. 64); indeed "you are obligated by the *most sacred ties*, to the fulfillment of these duties" (p. 65). "Duty and Honor bind" every Master Mason "to the furtherance of a strict obedience to the laws of Free Masonry" (p. 81). Such obedience "will convince the world that we deserve the blessings of our privileges." They declare that "only worthy men are admitted to their enjoyment, after they have taken a voluntary oath of allegiance" (p. 14). It is made known to the candidate, "that nothing will be required of him that could be an obstacle to his civil, moral, and religious obligations" (p. 14). Nothing more is required of him, as a matter of course, than that he should reject the word of God, deny Christ, give up his entire Christian belief and hold brotherly communication with unbelievers, in contradiction to the plain word of God (2 Cor. 6 : 14—18).

It is an important law of the Free Masons, to assist all the brothers. Hence all are admonished: "Remember, that you have laid upon this altar the solemn promise to support and assist *every brother* when he needs your aid" (p. 9). Because this is their duty, there is also a good reason for them to encourage the timid with the words: "Do not allow yourselves to be induced by *any-*

---

* See " Origin, Development and Signification of Secret Societies, by R. Clemen," p 77.

thing (therefore not even by the word of God) to deviate from your duties, to break your vows, or to betray the secrets entrusted to you" (p. 82). Christians however are instructed by the word of God, to break all sinful vows which they have made perhaps ignorantly. Dr. Luther says the same. Every "Master" must vow to honor and esteem the genuine and true brothers, on the contrary *to despise and to avoid* all deceivers and opostates from the original plan of Free Masonry" (p. 97. ff). He further promises "to avoid and to despise every person" who is admitted into a Lodge, which is in contradiction to his (p. 98). These gentlemen declare that every man who "does not endeavor to add to the universal treasures of science and enlightenment, may . . . . be considered unworthy of our protection as a Free Mason" (p. 76.) A fine universal love! The Lord Jesus teaches us not only to love "deceivers" and "apostates," but even our personal enemies. The Free Masons teach "to despise and to avoid" all such.

Free Masonry has also a great mission to fulfill. As it has placed itself *above* the word of God and the Christian religion, so "Free Masonry receives men of every land, of every sect, and opinion" (p. 29). And the more by 'wedging' are wedged in, the better. Their "System" is designed to "flourish and increase among all men on the face of the globe" (p. VI). What is the quintessence of their great mission? The "most important problem upon earth,—the preparation for eternity" (p. 124). Therefore they awaken "in the hearts of their disciples the knowledge of the great Architect of the universe" (p. VI). On p. VIII all are admonished : " Let us continually consider that the great aims of our brotherly covenant are : the control of improper desires and passions, the exercise of active benevolence and the obtaining of a true knowledge of the duties, which we owe to God, our neighbors, and ourselves." In this they of course have no need of the word of God. They will "follow the one aim" "to be kind to each other, and to unite for the great purpose of becoming happy, and *of creating and spreading* happiness *abroad"* (p. 108 ff.). In this they are conducted by the "good genius" of their "secret art" (p. VIII), and find the "sacred refuge of friendship and virtue" in their Lodge (p. IX). As they want to control "improper desires and passions," these must dwell in their hearts. What will they now do to get rid of them? That is to Free Masons a mere trifle. They declare on p. 16: "We use the hammer in the lodge, in order to purify our hearth and consciences from all the vices and follies of life and thereby to prepare our souls as living stones for that spiritual edifice . . . . in Heaven." To be sure, if the hammer has such power, the blood of Christ is to them the most superfluous thing in the world. In spite of their rejection of the living God and his word, they are still very pious people, for out of every twenty-four hours, they devote "eight hours to the service of God and of a needy brother" (p. 16). "To restore to the afflicted heart its lost rest and peace, is the great aim" that they follow (p. 29). This of course is not accomplished through the only prince of peace, but by the substitution of the thorny pillow of so-called good works. The hearts of all men, but particularly those of the "brothers," shall gradually be permeated "with the light of illumination" (p. 106). It is the duty of all, in thus warning against the kingdom of God, and by means of such antichristian and satanic doctrines "to create and spread happiness." And when the members labor zealously to disseminate their false doctrines, they are told: " Your work is done unto the Lord and your reward is with your God"! We believe this latter assertion fully; if they are not brought through the grace of God to upright repentance and conversion, THEIR GOD will in his own time give them a suitable "reward." In all that, the Free Mason must only take care that he does not violate the "Constitution," and that he acts only in accordance with the dictates of his perverted and darkened conscience. For on p. 26 it is said: "Let every Free Mason so regulate his actions as the voice of his conscience best teaches him."

The Order endeavors with all its might to promulgate all these false doctrines, and experience teaches that it succeeds in so doing In face of the great danger of being led astray by such unbelievers, we cannot urgently enough recommend to all Christians the faithful and diligent use of the blessed word of God, and not pressingly enough urge them to continually pray:

> "Thy Word is like a flaming sword,
> A wedge that cleaveth stone;
> Keen as a fire, so burns Thy Word,
> And pierceth flesh and bone.
> Let it go forth o'er all the earth,
> To cleanse our hearts within,
> To show Thy power in satan's hour,
> And break the might of sin."

CONCLUDING REMARKS.

It has not been in the remotest degree our intention, in setting forth the false doctrines of the secret societies, to wound the feelings of any one or do him wrong We have therefore strictly confined ourselves to the sources of our information and entirely set aside personal experience, as well as the experience of other Christians and congregations. That the picture which we gain, by personal experience of the doings of the members of secret societies is a thousand times more dreadful than that which the Order in its publications depicts of itself, is quite intelligible. The doctrines which they promulgate in their publications are, however, bad enough to keep every Christian, who has any concern for his soul's salvation, at a distance from the Lodge. And we would here most earnestly entreat every Christian not to suffer himself to be tempted to join, but to arm himself with the word of God and seriously contend against their false doctrines. But alas, many Christians and members of congregations are too little conversant with these doctrines, and it happens that they often are drawn into the Lodge by all manner of sweet sounding representations and phrases. The more so, as the members of the lodge do it in the most artful way. They never declare openly and intelligibly to all: "We will exterminate Christianity"; on the contrary, they frequently assume the appearance of great piety, and many a one thinks, "I will convince myself," and joins the lodge in order, as he thinks, to convince himself. And when he has been admitted, the standing phrase is: "I have neither seen nor heard anything evil." This may be in so far true, as that they have seen and heard nothing of so-called grave immoralities. The word of God, however (2 Cor. 6), has been transgressed. The lodge also suffers no new comers to look into its secret designs and plans, but uses them, unconscious to themselves, as tools, and only by degrees instils its false doctrines into them. Their eyes are darkened; they are gradually, without observing it, turned off from the word of God and the Church, become more indifferent to the preaching and the sacraments; the panegyrics and boasting of the many good works are sweet music to the natural heart, and the doctrine of being made good by our own virtues pleases more than repentance and faith, and so they are gradually, without knowing it, converted to the doctrine of the order. The forbidden communion with unbelievers exercises a fearful influence, and that is the reason why so few who have joined with the intention of investigating the subject, come to a perception of the false doctrines and withdraw from the lodge Before they have learned to know these by experience, they are usually long since "converted" to them. Is it, however, right for a Christian first to join and then to examine? First to transgress the word of God and enter into fellowship with unbelievers, and then to see and examine whether there is any-thing "evil" done there? No, assuredly not! Before we join a society and form a "brotherly alliance" with its members we must first examine their doctrine by the only correct standard, the sacred Scriptures. And whoever does so in good earnest, will, by the grace of God, be preserved from the poison of the doctrines of the lodge; and these doctrines are, God be praised, manifest, and no Christian can with a good conscience, promise obedience and secrecy, before he knows what will be required of him; but every one who is admitted, must do so.

The lodge, with its blasphemous doctrine, is a pestilence that walketh in darkness, a destruction that wasteth at noon-day. It is our ardent desire to help guard against it, and if any-one should have been captivated through ignorance, to assist him to come to the knowledge of the evil, this is our aim to which pure love compels us. To this end these lines were written. May it please the Lord to bless them to the souls of many!

www.ingramcontent.com/pod-product-compliance
Lightning Source LLC
Chambersburg PA
CBHW022112160426
43197CB00009B/986